AVOCA CAFÉ COOKBOOK

Editor Hugo Arnold   **Design** Vanessa Courtier   **Design assistant** Gina Hochstein   **Production** Tim Chester

Text © 2000 Hugo Arnold   Photography © 2000 Georgia Glynn Smith

The rights of Hugo Arnold to be identified as the Author of this Work has been asserted by him in accordance with the Copyright, Designs and Patents At 1988

First published in 2000 by Avoca Handweavers Ltd., Kilmacanogue, Bray, County Wicklow.

Reprinted in 2000, 2001 (four times), 2002 (three times), 2003 (four times), 2004 (twice), 2005 (three times), 2006 (twice), 2007 (twice), 2008 (twice), 2009 (twice), 2010 (twice), 2011

Printed and bound in Hong Kong by Great Wall Printing Company

Cataloguing-in-publication Data: a catalogue record for this book is available from the British Library   **ISBN 0-9538152-0-X**

AVOCA CAFÉ COOKBOOK

Written by Hugo Arnold with Leylie Hayes

Photography by Georgia Glynn Smith

CONTENTS

Avoca scones, page 143

ACKNOWLEDGEMENTS

Avoca is often credited as being one of the pioneers of modern Irish café food. The emphasis on a wide array of fresh salads, home-made soups, breads, cakes and tarts with a hint of whole food served in beautiful surroundings was an oasis in a sea of rather predictable pub and hotel lunches. If imitation is the highest form of flattery, then Avoca may blush as there have been many imitators. Although not rocket science, providing this standard of food does require passion, a refusal to compromise and a penchant for trying constantly to improve. While starting small, the leap came when Leylie Hayes joined the company. I owe an enormous amount to her enthusiasm, professionalism and utter commitment. Now executive chef of the cafés, she transformed our food into what it is today, much enlarged and with a consistency that is so vital.

I would like to say a special thank you to Teresa Byrne, now general manager of the cafés, whose amazing stewardship at Kilmacanogue has seen the café continue to improve. Her calmness and good humour, often in the face of considerable stress, is a wonder and delight to me. Nothing is too much trouble for Teresa and everything is done perfectly and finished yesterday.

My thanks also, to Michelle Collier who is a terrific head chef and a pleasure to work with and to her superb team in the kitchen at Kilmacanogue. Fleur Campbell, the self-taught patisserie perfectionist who works every hour God sends, and some He doesn't. And Eimer Rainsford, formerly head chef at Powerscourt, who recently launched the café in Dublin. In 1996 a glowing review of the Kilmacanogue café appeared in The Irish Times by John McKenna. His praise and understanding of what we were trying to do was a decided watershed in our development.

At Moll's Gap, Kathleen O'Sullivan and Anne Clifford who together with Mary and Hanna O'Sullivan under Eileen O'Leary 's watchful eye have made Moll's Gap Café so good. Mary T Mullin and Dympna Heanue under Maureen Walsh's guiding hand who have created such a welcoming tearoom at Letterfrack. Elizabeth Walker, who with her team, runs such a terrific operation in the café at the old mill in Avoca village. A big thank you to Mary Doyle and Valerie Hazlett, fantastic and ever reliable managers unstinting and unflappable in looking after one or 100 customers. To Catherine Darcy and Kate Redmond the wonderfully creative chefs.

From the early days, Yvonne Dixon, Jill Moss and my mother, Hilary Pratt (all superb cooks) have been a constant source of ideas, questions and comments that have kept us all on our toes. To my Dad and Des, for the magnificent gardens which always inspire and for the constant supply of fresh herbs. To Amanda and Tom for their creative input, to Ivan for always saying "Simon you should taste this, it's so good!" Catriona Lambe who meticulously typed and e-mailed all the recipes. To Hugo, Georgia and Vanessa for producing what I think is a beautiful book.

The cafés owe a huge debt to the loyalty of all our customers who seek us out, even when we are a bit off the beaten track and full to the rafters. And for your compliments, which keep us trying – thank you.

That the cafés have flourished is due to entirely to the staff who run them both past and present and the commitment you show to Avoca every day. There are simply too many wonderful people to name everyone, or to risk leaving anyone out. At the heart of the cafés is a culture I love – every day I overhear someone going the extra mile, be it in terms of customer service, or insisting that a dish isn't quite right yet, or taking on backbreaking manual wash-ups with good humour when a dishwasher breaks down. For me, this is what makes it all worthwhile.

Thank you everyone for all your individual contributions - this book is for you.

Simon Pratt

immorality of closing the mill. Charlie had a conscience about this and when in January 1974 Donald told him he was retiring from his legal practice, Charlie said: "You have lectured me enough about Avoca Handweavers, why don't you buy it and do all the things you say I should do?"

So on one cold wet miserable day in March 1974 the entire Pratt family descended on Avoca and through the teeming rain, tried to size up the possible usage. So struck were they by the idea that so much Irish heritage would disappear if the mill was closed, but with no clear idea what they might do with it themselves, they decided to buy. To give Charlie Holohan his due, he agreed a price of half what he thought the mill was worth. An act of folly? Hilary Pratt certainly doesn't think so now, but at the time it was all quite a risk.

Jim Barry was a key player in the saga. He ran the shop and, as Simon Pratt recounts, had a real passion for the mill. He once sold a sample of a particularly popular bedspread five times one day, promising each customer he would mail it to them and then putting it back up for sale when they had left. The following morning he was in the mill asking the weavers to weave replacements as soon as they could.

Jim Barry said to my father that if he reopened the mill he reckoned he could persuade all the weavers, then unhappily back in the mine, to come back to weaving. He was right. Within a few months the looms were all operational again, producing rugs and cloth with the Wynne sisters' unmistakable pinks, blues, purples and greens of the surrounding heather. Beautiful they may have been, but in order to survive they had to be sold.

Donald and his wife, Hilary, then a teacher, put some samples in the back of the car and headed to London, where they managed to sell a few into Harrods and Selfridges. It wasn't exactly plain sailing from then on, but the business grew steadily. Expansion came out of necessity, partly the need to find space, partly the need to open a site rather more convenient to Dublin than Avoca was in the depths of Wicklow.

There are a group of outbuildings at the bottom of the gardens at Kilmacanogue which are now the head offices. Back in the early Eighties the bottom storey held a workshop and the first floor housed a shop. In 1988 the company bought the adjoining 12 acres, on which one of the Jameson family, of whiskey fame, had built Glencormac house in the 1860s. Having become a hotel the house was completely destroyed by fire in 1967. On this site with its majestic gardens, by then completely overgrown, a new branch of Avoca was built.

Today it is twice its original size and in the summer the terrace adds substantially to the size of the café. Where once Avoca sold just throw rugs, tweeds and bedspreads, it now sells a vast range of items, from its chic Hope + Thimble clothing to books, children's wear to ceramics and take-away food from its new bakery. Customers are no longer only visitors seeking examples of classic Irish clothes, but Irish families and friends out shopping and walking and looking for somewhere to relax and enjoy lunch, a cup of coffee or afternoon tea on the beautiful terrace overlooking the now restored gardens.

The contemporary Hope and Thimble range was launched in 1999

Shops at Letterfrack in Connemara and Bunratty were added and in 1990 a shop opened in Annapolis in America, and in 1994 on Vancouver Island in Canada. Also in 1994, Avoca at Moll's Gap on the Ring of Kerry was opened in what was formerly Cremins, an outlet nestling in a dramatic pass, 1,000 feet above sea level on one of the most picturesque drives in the country. The view from the roof-top café has Carrauntoohill, the highest mountain in Ireland, on one side and the renowned Gap of Dunloe on the other.

In 1997 Avoca launched a large project, taking a lease over much of the ground floor of Powerscourt House, one of the finest Georgian houses in Ireland until it was tragically destroyed by fire in 1974. The house, still owned by the Slazenger family, is divided into an exhibition of the estate's wonderful history, and a number of different shopping areas culminating in the café looking out over Ireland's most famous gardens and the Wicklow hills

SOUPS

'It's the perfect lunch for me, good soup and Avoca brown bread. The variety of soup changes with the seasons, but it's always well made'

Petit pois and mint, page 21

Along with salads, soup remains one of the cornerstones of the Avoca cafés. In the early days, it was prepared and brought in by Simon Pratt. Then living in the gate lodge at Kilmacanogue, he spent his evenings cooking up large pots of minestrone and carrot soup, along with chicken liver pâté. In the morning he would load them into the back of his Renault van and take them to the shop to be heated up later in the day. "The idea was to do them the evening before so they could cool down but occasionally I left it until the following morning," he recalls. "Hot soup and cars don't mix, however, and one day the carrot soup spilt all over the floor. After that, not only was it time to change the car but we also realised the kitchen needed a more permanent home, and in a sense the cafés were born."

For Leylie Hayes, soup is one of the fundamentals of cooking." If you can make a good soup you have a wonderfully nourishing pot to sit around with friends and share. There may be nothing elaborate about it at all, but that is half the point. With home-made soup there is no pretension; it's honest, good food."

Leylie completed a one-year cookery course at Ballymaloe Cookery School and was then taken on at the hotel kitchen where her first job

Tomato, lentil and orange, page 20

was making soup. "It is a dish that is so easily thrown together and yet when made with care and patience can be sensational. It is one of the first things I get new chefs to do, how they go about soup making is generally illustrative of their whole approach."

The soups at Avoca are largely vegetarian. The occasional meat-based one appears on the menu in winter but this is unusual. They rarely include flour either, the addition of which is a common trick in catering to bulk out other ingredients.

Potato is also a common ingredient, used to make soups creamy in texture. We prefer, how-ever, to use real cream if we want creaminess.

For many, soup is a winter dish, something to warm you up, but not for warm summer months. Our soups are so popular, however, the idea of not having one is barely worth considering. Switch to lighter ingredients, serve them chilled and look to hot countries for inspiration, like the green bean and coconut on page 17.

We tend to purée soups in the café because it makes them easier and more con-sistent for serving. You can, however, leave them more chunky, which gives them a decidedly rustic, country feel.

Green bean and coconut

Outdoor eating is a passion for many and nowhere has it been more widely adopted than in Australia. This recipe (pictured opposite) was adapted from one Leylie Hayes came across while on holiday there. Back in Ireland, ingredients and cooking times were altered somewhat but in essence the soup is very Pacific Rim.

It needs to be prepared just before serving, since its colour does not hold for long. It is not suitable for freezing or the microwave. You could transform it into a curry with the addition of an extra chilli and some diced chicken breast. Alternatively, try a little nam pla (Thai fish sauce) and some prawns or monkfish.

Melt the butter in a large saucepan, add the spring onions, carrot, lemongrass, garlic and ginger and stir over a medium heat for 1 minute. Add the turmeric, coriander, chillies, green beans, coconut cream and stock cube and mix well. Bring to the boil, then reduce the heat and simmer, uncovered, for 5 minutes. Stir in the bean sprouts and fresh coriander, season to taste and serve.

15g/$\frac{1}{2}$oz butter

2 spring onions, chopped (including the green part)

1 medium carrot, cut into fine strips

2 teaspoons finely chopped lemongrass (dry outer layers removed first)

2 garlic cloves, peeled and crushed

1 teaspoon grated fresh ginger

1 teaspoon ground turmeric

2 teaspoons ground coriander

2 green chillies, chopped

12 green beans, roughly chopped

2 x 400ml/14fl oz cans of coconut cream

$\frac{1}{2}$ vegetable stock cube, crumbled (yes, even we use stock cubes on occasions)

110g/4oz bean sprouts

2 tablespoons chopped fresh coriander

'Ballymaloe taught me a great deal, but particularly about ingredients and the care and attention they demand. You can make a soup any old way, or you can do it properly and it makes all the difference in the world'

Courgette and almond

Melt the butter in a large pan, add the onion and potato and cook over a very low heat for 5 minutes. Add the stock, bring to the boil, then reduce the heat and simmer for 20 minutes or until the potato is cooked. Add the courgettes, bring back to the boil and simmer for 5 minutes. As soon as the courgettes are cooked, remove the pan from the heat and stir in the almonds, cream and milk. Purée in a blender, then reheat gently and season to taste. Serve topped with a few toasted flaked almonds and a swirl of cream.

15g/$\frac{1}{2}$oz butter
1 onion, peeled and chopped
1 potato, peeled and chopped
600ml/1 pint vegetable stock
3 courgettes, finely chopped
25g/1oz ground almonds
125ml/4fl oz double cream, plus
  extra to serve
125ml/4fl oz milk
Flaked almonds, to serve

Tomato, celery and apple

Some years ago there was a popular cabbage diet in Ireland, adopted by many and, not surprisingly, subsequently dropped. This soup was devised by a number of chefs heartily sick of cabbage. It is low in fat, but its popularity stems more from its delicacy and lightness, according to customers.

Cook the onion, celery and apple in the olive oil over a very low heat for 10 minutes. Add the tomatoes and stock and season with salt and pepper. Bring to the boil, then reduce the heat and simmer for 20 minutes. Purée in a blender, reheat gently and adjust the seasoning.

1 large onion, peeled and finely diced
$^1/_2$ head celery, finely diced
1 large cooking apple, peeled, cored and sliced
2 tablespoons olive oil
3 x 400g/14oz cans of chopped tomatoes
300ml/$^1/_2$ pint vegetable stock

Aztec corn

Corn was a staple part of the Aztec diet but its mealiness can become monotonous, hence the spices. South America is not renowned for its cuisine but this soup is deliciously simple, the lime giving it a delicate citrus lift at the end.

Melt the butter in a large pan, add the onions and sauté gently for 10 minutes, until translucent. Add the ground cumin and ground coriander and sauté for 2 minutes, stirring occasionally. Add the celery, sweetcorn, stock and some salt and pepper. Bring to the boil, then reduce the heat and simmer for 15 minutes. Purée the soup in a blender, then stir in the lime juice and zest and reheat gently. Adjust the seasoning and serve with the chopped coriander.

15g/$\frac{1}{2}$oz butter

2 large onions, peeled and finely chopped

4 rounded teaspoons ground cumin

1 rounded teaspoon ground coriander

$\frac{1}{2}$ head celery, finely chopped

1kg/2$\frac{1}{4}$lb canned or frozen sweetcorn, drained

1.2 litres/2 pints vegetable stock

Juice and grated zest of 1 lime

2 tablespoons chopped fresh coriander

Mixed mushroom

Melt the butter over a very low heat, add the onions and cook gently for 10 minutes or until translucent. Raise the heat, add the mushrooms and season well with salt and pepper. Cook for 3 minutes or until the juices start to run, then stir in the flour. Lower the heat and cook, stirring continuously, for about 8 minutes. Combine the stock and milk in a separate pan and bring to the boil, then remove from the heat. Gradually add the stock and milk to the mushroom mixture, whisking to avoid lumps. Heat the soup at just below simmering point for about 10 minutes, stirring occasionally. Add the thyme, check the seasoning and serve.

25g/1oz butter

450g/1lb onions, peeled and very finely chopped

1.1kg /2$\frac{1}{2}$lb mixed mushrooms, finely chopped

75g/3oz plain flour

1.2 litres/2 pints vegetable stock

600ml/1 pint full-cream milk

1 teaspoon chopped fresh thyme

Sweet potato and lemongrass

Living in a country with a history as steeped in the potato as Ireland, it was hard to resist playing around with the sweet variety, according to Leylie Hayes. The original dish was more of a curry, a fusion of East and West, which was transformed into a soup.

Sweat the onions and potatoes in the butter over a very low heat for 5 minutes. Add the sweet potatoes and stir to coat them in the butter. Pour in the stock, bring to the boil, then reduce the heat and simmer for 30 minutes. Meanwhile, remove the dry outer layers of the lemongrass and finely chop the moist interior. Cover with boiling water and leave for 10 minutes, then add the lemongrass and its soaking water to the soup. Purée in a blender, then reheat and season to taste.

700g/1 ½ lb onions, peeled and chopped
225g/8oz potatoes, peeled and chopped
50g/2oz butter
700g/1 ½ lb sweet potatoes, peeled and chopped
1.8 litres/3 pints vegetable stock
6–8 lemongrass stalks

Potato and fennel

Fennel is a winter rather than a summer vegetable, eaten at the same time as hearty, cold-weather dishes despite its rather bright aniseed flavour. This soup is for just those colder months, in reality rather more predominant in Ireland than in Italy.

Sweat the onion and potatoes in the butter over a very low heat for 10 minutes, stirring occasionally to prevent sticking. Add the fennel, stock and some salt and pepper and bring to the boil, then reduce the heat and simmer for 20 minutes. Purée in a blender, then stir in the milk and reheat gently. Adjust the seasoning and serve.

1 onion, peeled and diced
2 large potatoes, peeled and diced
15g/½ oz butter
4 fennel bulbs, thinly sliced
1.2 litres/2 pints vegetable stock
300ml/½ pint full-cream milk

SALADS

'I'm hardly vegetarian, but there is something about the salads at Avoca which means they are inevitably what I have. I cannot resist them'

Broccoli, feta, hazelnut and cherry tomato, page 37

Stop for lunch on a summer's day at any of the Avoca shops and much of the focus will be on salads. Sometimes there are as many as 15. All will have been made that morning, from ingredients that even a few years ago would have been hard to obtain. Fresh herbs, to start with: the fiery, aniseed taste of tarragon, peppery mint and sweet, fragrant basil are partnered with red, sun-ripened tomatoes, pungent radishes and cooling cucumber and courgettes. The courgettes might be grated and mixed with carrots, coriander, poppy seeds and a vinaigrette where orange takes the place of vinegar; tomatoes, this time cherry and honey sweet, are combined with broccoli, feta and toasted hazelnuts; while cucumber might be dressed with yoghurt, garlic and mint, its crunch and freshness just the thing to soothe away the heat of the day.

In winter, too, people seek out salads, often to partner soup for an informal lunch. Here root vegetables shine – beetroot, perhaps, tossed with toasted almonds and coated with more yoghurt; or celeriac, fashioned into rémoulade with carrot, flat-leaf parsley and a rich, full-bodied home-made mayonnaise. Potatoes are sautéed with garlic and rosemary and tossed in balsamic vinegar. In winter couscous is made with root vegetables, as in North Africa, but when

Red cabbage with bacon and red onion, page 49

the summer sun shines, red peppers and other summer vegetables are used. While Italians may consider that salad is green leaves and olive oil, at Avoca salads have become something of an art form.

How do we invent them? Many are born from necessity, as has been the case for much of Ireland's culinary history. Whereas in the past dishes were concocted around turf fires from whatever was available, at Avoca our inventive spirit is often sparked off by queues of hungry customers. Our beetroot salad, for example, emerged from a busy bank holiday weekend when the cry for more salad was met by silence from the kitchen – we were out of fresh vegetables. Somebody remembered the beetroot, somebody else the yoghurt and a new dish was born.

The recipes in this chapter are very much a guide – do not be a slave and buy carrots when you'd rather leave them where they are. Invent something new and celebrate the change. Unlike desserts, where amounts and ingredients are often crucial, here you can be more of a free spirit, let rip and give it a go.

Salads are all about freshness and don't be too tempted to gild the lily – simplicity is key to a successful salad.

Carrot and courgette

This is an adaptation of the carrot and roasted sesame seed salad below.

Put the grated carrots and courgettes in a bowl and mix with the coriander, French dressing, seeds, orange juice and most of the grated zest. Season to taste. Garnish with the remaining orange zest and a sprig of coriander.

5 carrots, peeled and coarsely
  grated
5 courgettes, coarsely grated
A bunch of fresh coriander,
  chopped (reserve a sprig
  for garnish)
4 tablespoons French dressing
  (see page 180)
1 dessertspoon roasted
  pumpkin seeds
  (see page 185)
1 dessertspoon poppy seeds
Juice of 1 orange
Grated zest of 2 oranges

Carrot with roasted sesame seeds

Simple and full of colour, this is a combination that works so well it seems as classic as Caesar or niçoise. The carrot's pedigree is important; choose organic if possible and nothing too old. Crunch and a good colour are essential. Lacklustre specimens need not apply. As far as quantities are concerned, this salad should be made to taste. As a guide, use about a tablespoon of sesame seeds to 5 large carrots. You could use other seeds such as poppy, pumpkin or linseeds, or substitute pine nuts.

Roast the sesame seeds in a dry frying pan (see page 185). Add them to the grated carrot and toss with 3 tablespoons of French dressing. Check the seasoning and serve.

1 dessertspoon sesame seeds
4 coarsely grated carrots
French dressing
  (see page 180)

'The most popular Avoca salad? Broccoli, cherry tomato, feta and toasted hazelnut'

Beetroot, almond and yoghurt

If it is the sharpness of beetroot that puts you off, try this salad; the yoghurt and almonds make it far more mellow and give it a rounded, full flavour.

Combine the beetroot, yoghurt and two-thirds of the almonds in a bowl. Garnish with the remaining almonds.

1kg/2¼lb pickled sliced beet-
    root, drained
350g/12oz Greek-style yoghurt
50g/2oz flaked almonds, toasted
    (see page 185)

Cauliflower, broccoli and roasted monkey nuts

Cut the cauliflower and broccoli into florets of equal size. Toast the peanuts in the oven until golden. Add the peanuts to the cauliflower and coat with the yoghurt dressing. Season with salt and pepper and serve.

1 medium-sized cauliflower
1 good-sized stalk of broccoli
110g/4oz monkey nuts
Greek yoghurt dressing
   (see page 180)

Broccoli, feta, hazelnut and cherry tomato

Toast the hazelnuts in a hot oven (see page 185), then tip them into a tea towel and rub off the skins. Allow to cool, then put the hazelnuts in a bowl with the broccoli, cheese and cherry tomatoes. Gently toss with the dressing and season with pepper. Salt may not be required, since the feta is usually salty enough.

110g/4oz hazelnuts
400g/14oz broccoli florets
   (bite-sized)
110g/4oz feta cheese, cut into
   bite-sized cubes
225g/8oz cherry tomatoes,
   halved
200ml/7 fl oz French dressing
   (see page 180)

Potato and mint

As classic as they come. Buy the best potatoes you can and leave the rest to nature. And don't skimp on the salt. This is not the time to be worrying about over-indulgence; reserve that for the next time you are tempted by a packet of crisps.

Place the potatoes in a pan of salted water and bring to the boil. Simmer for about 15 minutes or until tender, then drain and place in a bowl. Mix with the French dressing and leave to cool. Mix the mayonnaise, yoghurt and mint together and pour over the potatoes. Season with salt and pepper and serve.

900g/2lb small new potatoes
2 tablespoons French dressing
   (see page 180)
6 tablespoons mayonnaise
2 tablespoons plain yoghurt
A large bunch of mint, chopped

Roast herbed potato with balsamic vinegar

Although it is served in the cafés as a salad, this dish originated as an accompaniment to roast beef in place of ordinary roast potatoes. Turning it into a salad required some fine tuning but it has emerged as one of the most popular. 'I think there is something inherently Irish about eating potatoes,' says Simon.

Dry the diced potatoes in a clean tea towel and toss them generously in olive oil. Spread them out in an ovenproof dish (it should not be too crowded) and roast for 10 minutes in an oven preheated to 220°C/425°F/gas mark 7. Add the garlic and half the herbs and continue to roast for a further 10–15 minutes, until the potatoes and garlic are tender. Remove from the oven. Allow to cool slightly, then add more olive oil to taste, sprinkle with balsamic or red wine vinegar and add the remaining herbs. Check the seasoning and serve.

1.8kg/4lb potatoes, diced
  (skin left on)
Olive oil
1 head of garlic, split into cloves
  but left unpeeled
1 tablespoon finely chopped
  fresh rosemary
1 tablespoon finely chopped
  fresh thyme
Balsamic vinegar or good-quality
  red wine vinegar

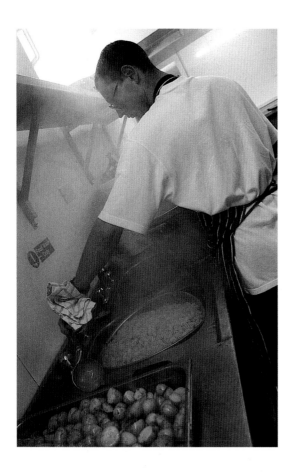

Spinach, sun-dried tomato, Parmesan, pine nuts and pasta

This recipe can be used as a dressing for hot pasta, which was where Eimer got the original idea. Do use the best olive oil you can; it is integral to the dish.

Cook the pasta in boiling salted water until tender, then drain. Add all the remaining ingredients except the spinach, mix well and season to taste. Leave to cool, then add the spinach.

500g/18oz pasta (penne or fusilli)

4 tablespoons freshly grated Parmesan cheese

2 tablespoons pine nuts, toasted (see page 185)

3 tablespoons roughly chopped semi sun-dried tomatoes, together with their oil

125ml/4fl oz best-quality extra virgin olive oil

175g/6oz baby spinach leaves, shredded

Smoked bacon, blue cheese and pineapple pasta

Cook the pasta in boiling salted water until tender, then drain. Cut the bacon into bite-sized pieces and fry in a dry frying pan until very crisp, then drain on kitchen paper and set aside. Place the pasta, bacon, mangetout, spinach, pineapple pieces (reserving the juice) and almonds in a bowl. Blend together the blue cheese, yoghurt, mayonnaise and the juice from the canned pineapple to make a dressing. Toss the pasta with the dressing and season, but be cautious with the salt; the bacon may well be salty enough. Garnish with some chopped chives and a few toasted flaked almonds.

500g/18oz penne
225g/8oz smoked bacon
110g/4oz mangetout, cut into
    narrow strips
50g/2oz baby spinach leaves,
    shredded
200g/7oz can of pineapple
50g/2oz flaked almonds, toasted
    (see page 185), plus a few
    extra to garnish
110g/4oz Cashel Blue or other
    blue cheese, crumbled
110g/4oz Greek-style yoghurt
110g/4oz mayonnaise
Chopped fresh chives, to garnish

Tuna, fusilli, mixed pepper

Cook the pasta in boiling salted water until tender, then drain and place in a mixing bowl. While still warm, toss with the French dressing and season to taste. Leave to cool, then add the tuna, peppers, spring onions and tomatoes. Mix well and check the seasoning. Garnish with the olives and basil leaves.

1kg/2$\frac{1}{4}$lb fusilli
200ml/7fl oz French dressing
    (see page 180)
225g/8oz canned tuna in oil,
    drained
2 large red and 2 large yellow
    peppers, deseeded and finely
    diced
1 large bunch of spring onions,
    thinly sliced
2 tablespoons roughly chopped
    semi sun-dried tomatoes
2 tablespoons roughly chopped
    black olives
A handful of torn basil leaves

Overleaf from left: Beetroot, almond and yoghurt (page 36), Roasted herbed potato with balsamic vinegar (page 38), Carrot and courgette (page 35), Broccoli, feta, hazelnut and cherry tomato (page 37)

Kilmacanogue curried rice

Michelle's mother developed this salad for picnics on the beaches of Wexford. According to Michelle, the sun always shone, but then, as she points out, it always does when you are a child.

Cook the rice in boiling salted water until tender, then drain. Lightly toast the curry powder and turmeric in a dry frying pan. Add to the rice along with all the other ingredients. Toss lightly, then season to taste. Try not to handle the rice too much or it will become sticky.

450g/1lb long grain rice
$\frac{1}{2}$ teaspoon curry powder
    (Madras mild)
$\frac{1}{2}$ teaspoon turmeric
75g/3oz sultanas
75g/3oz no-need-to-soak dried
    apricots, chopped
285g/10oz can of sweetcorn,
    drained
110g/4oz frozen petits pois,
    thawed
125ml/4fl oz lemon juice
1 teaspoon olive oil

Triple rice salad with sesame dressing

Cook each type of rice in a separate pan of boiling salted water until just tender, then drain. Place in a large mixing bowl, add the sesame oil and olive oil and season to taste. Leave to cool, then stir in the peppers, mangetout, peas and herbs. Check the seasoning and serve.

700g/1$\frac{1}{2}$lb basmati rice
150g/5oz wild rice
150g/5oz wahini/red rice
200ml/7fl oz sesame oil
100ml/3$\frac{1}{2}$fl oz olive oil
2 large red and 2 large yellow
    peppers, finely diced
110g/4oz mangetout, thinly
    sliced
175g/6oz frozen petits pois,
    thawed
50g/2oz fresh mint leaves,
    chopped
50g/2oz fresh flat-leaf parsley,
    chopped

Oriental bean sprout and egg noodle

This is Amanda Pratt's favourite salad. A lunch of this is the perfect break in a day dominated by material and designs. Most of the clothes at Avoca are either designed or overseen by Amanda, or her mother, Hilary. 'I need something refreshing and different as an antidote,' she says, 'and this is perfect.'

Gently heat the sesame oil in a frying pan, taking care not to let it burn; this can easily happen, as sesame oil burns at quite a low temperature. Add the garlic and ginger and sauté gently for 2 minutes or until lightly golden. Stir in the soy sauce and allow to cool.

Cook the egg noodles according to the instructions on the packet. Drain well, add them to the sesame oil and soy mixture and leave to cool. Mix all the vegetables and the bean sprouts with the cooled noodles, along with any of the optional additions.

Optional additions
Roasted peanuts, water chestnuts, diced cooked chicken breast, cooked prawns.

5 tablespoons sesame oil

3 garlic cloves, peeled and finely chopped

2cm/$\frac{3}{4}$ inch piece of fresh ginger, peeled and finely chopped

6 tablespoons soy sauce

40g/1$\frac{1}{2}$oz egg thread noodles

1 yellow and 2 red peppers, cut into strips

110g/4oz mangetout, blanched, refreshed and cut into strips, or 110g/4oz broccoli florets, blanched and refreshed

A bunch of spring onions, trimmed and sliced at an angle

700g/1$\frac{1}{2}$lb bean sprouts

Red cabbage with bacon and red onion

This salad is popular for its crunchy texture and bright colour and is often mistaken for beetroot. The colour is certainly striking and makes a good contrast to many other recipes in this chapter, so it is particularly suitable for a buffet.

Place the shredded cabbage in a bowl. Put the honey and vinegar in a pan and heat until the honey has melted. Pour this mixture over the cabbage. Cover and leave to marinate for at least 4–5 hours, preferably overnight.

Put the onions and salt in a sieve, toss well and set aside for 10 minutes (this reduces the strength of the onions somewhat). Rinse thoroughly and pat dry.

Sauté the bacon in a dry frying pan until very crisp. Add it to the cabbage with the sliced onions, season and serve.

1 red cabbage, outer leaves and core removed, finely shredded
3 tablespoons runny honey
125ml/4fl oz red wine vinegar
3 red onions, peeled and thinly sliced
1 tablespoon salt
225g/8oz bacon, cut into lardons

Butterbean, smoked bacon and garlic

Soak the beans overnight in plenty of cold water. Rinse well, cover with fresh water and cook for 45 minutes to 1 hour, the timing will depend on the age of the beans. Drain and dress the beans while warm with the remaining ingredients, check seasoning and serve.

450g/1lb butterbeans
110g/4oz crispy lardons of smokey bacon
2 garlic cloves, crushed
2 lemons
8 tablespoons olive oil
A bunch of flat-leaf parsley, chopped

Avoca's three-bean

To make the dressing, combine the mustard and garlic in a large bowl, season with salt and pepper and then gradually whisk in the olive oil. Add the lemon juice to taste.

Stir the beans and vegetables into the dressing and mix well. Taste and adjust the seasoning.

400g/14oz can each of kidney beans, chickpeas and butter-beans, drained and well rinsed

4 spring onions, finely chopped

2 red and 2 yellow peppers, diced

1 small can of sweetcorn, drained and well rinsed

For the dressing

1 tablespoon Dijon mustard

3 garlic cloves, peeled, chopped and mashed to a paste with a little salt, using the flat of a large knife

125ml/4fl oz extra virgin olive oil

Juice of 1 lemon

The mill at Avoca, the terrace at Kilmacanogue

Summer fruit salad

Peel, deseed and dice the melon and mix with all the remaining ingredients in a large bowl, then taste and add more sugar if necessary. You can add some Pimms or Cointreau to this, which gives it a little more punch.

1.3kg/3lb ripe Galia melon

2 large oranges, zested, peeled and segmented

2 large nectarines, skinned, stoned and thinly sliced

1 punnet of strawberries, hulled and cut in half

1 cucumber, halved lengthways, deseeded and sliced

3 tablespoons chopped fresh mint

2 teaspoons icing sugar

Summer fruit salad

Fish pie

This recipe comes in many forms and often a great deal is included, from oysters to prawns, from mushrooms to peas. In essence, it is a winter dish, something to be enjoyed while the wind roars and howls outside. You can add whatever ingredients you want, but too many additions confuse the tastebuds. Use restraint and your guests are more likely to be impressed.

We are often asked what to serve with fish pie. A baked potato is good, unless the pie has a potato topping, but after that a green salad is all you are likely to require.

Put the haddock in a saucepan with the onions, milk, bay leaf and peppercorns. Place over a moderate heat, bring slowly to the boil and poach the fish for 5 minutes, or until it flakes easily. Remove the fish and set aside to cool, reserving the cooking liquid.

Gently melt the butter in a saucepan and whisk in the flour. Strain the reserved milk from cooking the fish and gradually stir it into the roux. Bring to a simmer and cook for 5 minutes, stirring all the time. Season with salt and pepper.

Break the fish up into large chunks and place in a shallow oven-proof dish. Add the hardboiled eggs, parsley and peas and pour the sauce on top. Scatter over the breadcrumbs and dot generously with butter. Bake in an oven preheated to 180°C/350°F/gas mark 4 for 30–40 minutes, until brown and bubbling.

700g/1 ½ lb smoked haddock
2 onions, peeled and chopped
600ml/1 pint full-cream milk
1 bay leaf
10 black peppercorns
110g/4oz butter, plus extra for
  the topping
50g/2oz plain flour
4 eggs, hardboiled, shelled and
  halved
A bunch of flat-leaf parsley,
  chopped
200g/7oz frozen peas
6 tablespoons breadcrumbs

Herb-crusted cod

Mix together the breadcrumbs, garlic and herbs. Season the fish pieces with salt and pepper, then lightly coat them in the oil. Roll the fish in the breadcrumb mixture, gently pressing it into the flesh. Place on a baking tray and cook in an oven preheated to 200°C/400°F/gas mark 6 for 15 minutes or until the fish is cooked through.

3 tablespoons breadcrumbs

1 garlic clove, peeled, chopped and crushed with a little salt, using the flat of a large knife

3 tablespoons chopped mixed fresh herbs, such as thyme, parsley, chervil, dill and chives

4 pieces of cod fillet, about 175g/6oz each, skinned

2 tablespoons olive oil

Asian-style crabcakes with fruit chutney

This recipe was developed for a cookery demonstration on an East-meets-West theme, and may be served as a starter or a canapé. The demonstration was given by Eimer, complete with peaked cap. which can be spotted in photographs in this book. She claims only to own three, but current estimates run to two dozen.

For the chutney, put all the ingredients in a small pan and cook for 15 minutes over a low heat, stirring regularly, until the mixture thickens to a chutney consistency. Be careful not to let it darken too much. Leave to cool and then chill.

For the crabcakes, put the first eight ingredients in a bowl and whisk together well. Lightly whisk the egg white and cornflour together and fold into the crab and prawn mixture. Shape into small cakes, or tiny ones for canapés. Shallow-fry in hot vegetable oil for 2–3 minutes on each side, until golden brown. Serve straight away.

225g/8oz cooked white crab meat, well drained

8 raw prawns, shelled and chopped

2 spring onions, finely sliced

2 dashes of light soy sauce

2 green chillies, deseeded and finely chopped

A bunch of coriander, leaves and stalks chopped together

2 lemongrass stalks, dry outer layers removed, inner core finely chopped

1 teaspoon fish sauce

1 medium egg white

1 dessertspoon cornflour

Vegetable oil for shallow-frying

For the chutney

1 slice of pineapple, finely diced

½ mango, finely diced

½ pawpaw, finely diced

2.5cm/1 inch piece of fresh ginger, finely grated

1 garlic clove, peeled and crushed

½ small red onion, peeled and finely diced

2 tablespoons red wine vinegar

1 tablespoon soft brown sugar

Ground cloves and cumin, to taste

Makes about 30

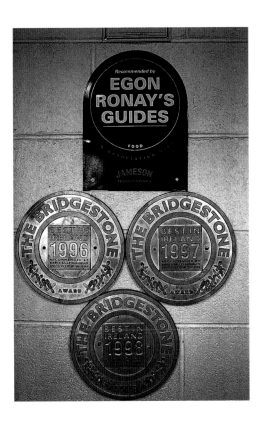

Eimer's spinach, chicken and crème fraîche filo parcels

Filo pastry is one of the few prepared things brought into the café kitchens; we make practically every-thing else. Getting filo to the correct thinness can be time consuming, and commercial brands are extremely good. These filo parcels are served as a main course at Powerscourt but smaller ones make good canapés. You could use smoked chicken.

Wash the spinach, removing any tough stalks, then put it in a saucepan with just the water clinging to its leaves and cook until wilted. Drain well. Put it in a food processor with the spring onions, cooked chicken, crème fraîche and tarragon and blitz to a purée. The mixture should not be totally smooth. Add the pine nuts and season to taste with the nutmeg and some salt and pepper.

Cut the sheets of filo into strips about 13cm/5 inches wide, or 6cm/2½ inches wide if you are making canapés. Brush one strip with melted butter and top with a second sheet (keep the remaining filo covered with a damp tea towel so it won't dry out). Place a small dollop of the filling about 2.5cm/1 inch from the top and fold the top left-hand corner down over it so it meets the right-hand edge. Now flip the parcel along the length of the filo to give a triangle-shaped package. Brush with melted butter. Repeat with the remaining filo and filling. Place the filo parcels on a greased baking sheet and bake in an oven preheated to 180°C/350°F/gas mark 4 for 20 minutes or until golden.

450g/1lb fresh spinach
10 spring onions, finely chopped
900g/2lb cooked chicken
700g/1½lb crème fraîche
1 tablespoon chopped fresh
  tarragon
½ cup pine nuts, toasted
  (see page 185)
A pinch of freshly grated nutmeg
1 packet of filo pastry
110g/4oz butter, melted

Chicken marinated in honey and mustard

Marinades bring complexity and richness to meat. Honey and mustard was one of the earliest tried in the café and it remains as popular as ever. The alternatives given below were designed with chicken in mind but they also work with quail, guinea fowl and lamb. Serve hot with fragrant rice or cold with salads.

Combine the honey, mustard, lemon juice and a generous seasoning of black pepper in a bowl. Add the chicken pieces, turn them over to coat in the marinade, then cover and leave to marinate in the fridge overnight.

The next day, transfer the chicken and marinade to a roasting tin and bake in an oven preheated to 180°C/350°F/gas mark 4 for 25 minutes or until the chicken is cooked through. Remove the chicken from the tin and keep warm. Place the roasting tin over a moderate heat and simmer until the sauce has a syrupy consistency. Serve with the chicken.

225g/8oz honey
2 tablespoons wholegrain
   mustard
Juice of 3 large lemons
8 chicken breasts
Serves 8

Variations

Rosemary and garlic marinade
1 tablespoon chopped fresh rosemary
2 garlic cloves, peeled and finely chopped
1 shallot, peeled and finely chopped
Juice of 1 lemon, plus the skin, roughly chopped
Olive oil

Combine the first 4 ingredients, then whisk in enough olive oil to form a sauce. Spread over chicken or lamb and set aside for a few hours to marinate.

Soy and ginger marinade
2 tablespoons soy sauce
3cm/1¼ inch piece of fresh ginger, peeled and finely chopped
1 red chilli, finely chopped
1 dessertspoon honey
1 dessertspoon nam pla (Thai fish sauce)
1 dessertspoon medium sherry
Vegetable oil

Combine the first 6 ingredients, then whisk in enough vegetable oil to form a sauce. Spread over chosen meat and set aside for a few hours to marinate.

'I could eat this gratin for ever; good, simple home-style cookery, with all the ingredients tasting of themselves'

Chicken and broccoli gratin

Place the chicken in a large saucepan with the onion, carrots, celery, parsley, bay leaf, peppercorns and enough water to cover. Bring slowly to the boil, then reduce the heat and simmer until the chicken is cooked – about an hour for a whole chicken, 20 minutes for chicken breasts. Remove the chicken from the pan and leave to cool. Strip the meat off the bones, dice and set aside.

Strain the cooking liquid into a saucepan and boil until reduced to 600ml/1 pint. Add the cream, return to the boil and then whisk in the roux a little at a time to form a thick sauce.

Blanch the broccoli in boiling salted water until just tender, then drain and refresh under cold water. Stir the diced chicken and broccoli into the sauce and season to taste with salt and pepper. Pour this mixture into an ovenproof dish. Melt the butter and mix with the cheese and the breadcrumbs. Spread over the chicken mixture and bake in an oven preheated to 180°C/350°F/gas mark 4 for 20 minutes or until brown and bubbling.

6 chicken breasts or 1 whole chicken

1 Spanish onion, peeled and chopped

2 carrots, peeled and chopped

2 celery sticks, chopped

A few sprigs of parsley

1 bay leaf

A few black peppercorns

300ml/$\frac{1}{2}$ pint double cream

110g/4oz roux (see page 184)

1 large head of broccoli, divided into florets

15g/$\frac{1}{2}$oz butter

50g/2oz strong cheese, grated

110g/4oz breadcrumbs

MEAT

'If I come to Kilmacanogue for lunch it always turns into the main meal of the day for me. I cannot resist the stews and casseroles'

Beef and Guinness stew, page 81

As a nation we talk endlessly about the weather, but can you blame us? It is never the same, changing from pouring rain to stunning sunshine in a matter of minutes. The variety, however, is one of the reasons our meat is so good. We have some of the best grassland in Europe and our climate means the meat has plenty of fat covering so necessary for flavour.

At Avoca we generally use the more succulent cuts of meat in our dishes, designed as they are for service in the cafés. We don't go in for short-order cooking. Instead our meat dishes tend to be braised long and slowly, so all the flavours amalgamate gently over time. The added advantage of this for the home cook is that these are dishes that can largely be prepared ahead, then reheated when you need them. This allows the flavours to develop and there are many who say a slowly cooked dish is even better the following day.

The influences for these recipes come from far and wide. We could hardly omit Irish stew, but chefs' travels in South America, India, the European mainland and Asia have all contributed. Ten years ago this chapter would more than likely have been composed of Irish-inspired stews and casseroles. That it now features curries, Italian-inspired dishes and modern twists

Pork and chicken terrine, page 93

on old themes, such as the Lakeshore pork on page 96, only goes to illustrate how much has happened over the last few years.

We were very much a society of meat and two vegetables but a great deal has changed in the recent past. No longer are people inclined to pile their plates high with thick slices of beef, pork and lamb. They are far more likely to eat meat less often, but spend more money and time on it when they do.

This approach has resulted in better meat, with much more attention being paid to fat covering, aging and breed, which all ultimately influence the final result.

When shopping for meat, consider for a moment the life the animal has led and look again at the price. We pay surprisingly little for meat, given the work, time and effort that goes into its production and where once our choice was limited, there is now everything from organic to free-range and a whole host of in-between categories. On the whole you get pretty much what you pay for, something dry and stringy, or alternatively something moist, succulent and full of flavour.

Long slow cooking is required, Irish time – in other words, getting there is equally as important as arriving.

Baked lamb with oven-roasted Mediterranean vegetables

Trim the lamb and cut into bite-sized cubes. Toss in the cornflour with a generous grinding of black pepper. In a flameproof casserole, brown the meat in small batches in some olive oil and set aside. In the casserole, sauté the onions in 4 tablespoons of olive oil for 10 minutes without colouring. Add the garlic and cook for 2 minutes. Return the meat to the pan with the herbs, tomatoes, sugar and red wine. Bring to the boil, then place, uncovered, in an oven preheated to 200°C/400°F/gas mark 6. Cook for 40 minutes or until the lamb is tender. Shortly before the end of the cooking time, toss the peppers, courgette and aubergine lightly in olive oil, place on a baking sheet and roast in the oven for 10 minutes. Combine with the meat and serve.

1.3kg/3lb leg of lamb
2 tablespoons cornflour
Olive oil
2 onions, peeled and diced
4 garlic cloves, peeled and finely chopped
A bunch of oregano, chopped
A bunch of marjoram, chopped
450g/1lb tomatoes, chopped
2 tablespoons sugar
200ml/7fl oz red wine
1 red and 1 yellow pepper, chopped
1 courgette, chopped
1 aubergine, chopped
Serves 6

Avoca's Irish stew

Lightly brown the chops in a frying pan and then place in a large flameproof casserole dish. Toss the onions and carrots in any remaining fat in the pan and add to the casserole. Cover with the stock, season well and place the potatoes on top. Bake in an oven preheated to 180°C/350°F/gas mark 4 for about 1 1/4 hours, until the vegetables are cooked and the meat is tender. Remove from the oven, take the meat and vegetables out of the casserole and keep warm. Put the casserole on the stove and bring the liquid to the boil. Whisk in the flour and butter mixture, a teaspoon at a time, to thicken. Check the seasoning and return the meat and vegetables to the dish along with the herbs. Reheat gently and serve.

8 large gigot lamb chops
16 small pearl onions, peeled but left whole
8 medium carrots, peeled and cut into 4cm/1 1/2 inch chunks
900ml/2 pints good-quality chicken or lamb stock
8 large potatoes, peeled but left whole
1 tablespoon each of flour and butter combined
1 tablespoon chopped fresh thyme
1 tablespoon chopped fresh flat-leaf parsley
1 tablespoon chopped fresh chives

Santa Fé pork stew

Ideas for recipes come from many sources. This one originally came from an American cookbook called The New Basics Cookbook by Julee Rosso and Sheila Lukins. Over time, it evolved into its current format.

Toss the pork in the seasoned flour. In a flameproof casserole, brown the meat in small batches in some olive oil and set aside. In the casserole, gently sauté the onions in 4 tablespoons of olive oil for 10 minutes or until opaque. Add the garlic, cumin and chilli and cook for 3–4 minutes. Return the pork to the casserole, add the tomatoes, white wine, stock and vinegar and season with salt and pepper. Bring to the boil, then transfer to an oven preheated to 180°C/350°F/gas mark 4 and cook, uncovered, for 30 minutes. Remove from the oven and add the sweet potatoes, then return to the oven for 30 minutes. Remove again, add the beans and cook for a further 15 minutes, until the beans are warmed through. Stir in the chopped coriander and parsley and serve with crème fraîche and lime wedges.

1.3kg/3lb leg of pork, diced
2½ tablespoons flour or cornflour, generously seasoned with
   salt and pepper
Olive oil
2 large onions, peeled and finely
   chopped
6 garlic cloves, peeled and
   crushed
1½ tablespoons ground cumin
1 green chilli, finely chopped
400g/14oz can of tomatoes
300ml/½ pint white wine
300ml/½ pint chicken stock
125ml/4fl oz red wine vinegar
2 large sweet potatoes, peeled
   and cut into 2.5cm/1 inch
   cubes
400g/14oz can of black or red
   kidney beans, drained
½ cup chopped fresh coriander
½ cup chopped fresh flat-leaf
   parsley
Crème fraîche and lime wedges
   to serve

Pork and chicken terrine

From a chef's perspective, it is curious what sells and what doesn't. When we put pork terrine on the menu it wasn't especially popular until, in a burst of inspiration, Leylie decided to include apricot and chicken in it. Some dishes are like this – inherently good but they somehow fail to catch the customers' imagination and yet with small changes they walk out the door.

This terrine is particularly good for picnics with brown bread and chutney, which was one of the reasons behind developing the picnic concept at Kilmacanogue: buy your lunch, borrow a rug and some glasses and enjoy the extensive gardens.

Sweat the onion in the butter over a low heat until opaque. Add the garlic and chopped herbs, cook for 2 minutes, then leave to cool.

Line a 900g/2lb loaf tin with the smoked bacon rashers, reserving a few to cover the top. Put the minced belly pork, minced bacon, cooled onion mixture, eggs, brandy, spinach, nuts and half the apricots in a large bowl and mix thoroughly. Season well with freshly ground black pepper (salt may not be necessary because the bacon is salty), then fry a small amount, taste and check the seasoning. Add salt to the mixture if required.

Place half the mixture in the lined tin, layer the thinly sliced chicken on top and then put the remaining apricots on top of that. Add the remaining meat mixture and cover with the remaining smoked bacon rashers and the bay leaf. Cover with foil, place in a roasting tin of hot water and bake for 1 hour in an oven preheated to 170°C/325°F/gas mark 3. Uncover and bake for a further 15 minutes. To check if the terrine is done, pierce the centre with a skewer and see if the juices run clear. It can be served hot or cold, although it is more difficult to slice when hot.

1 onion, peeled and finely
   chopped
25g/1oz butter
4 garlic cloves, peeled and
   crushed
A handful of mixed fresh herbs,
   such as thyme, rosemary, sage
   and marjoram, chopped
10 rindless smoked bacon
   rashers
700g/1 $\frac{1}{2}$lb fatty belly pork,
   minced
225g/8oz streaky bacon, minced
2 eggs
100ml/3 $\frac{1}{2}$fl oz brandy
175g/6oz baby spinach leaves,
   shredded
2 handfuls of pistachio nuts
175g/6oz no-need-to-soak dried
   apricots
1 skinless, boneless chicken
   breast, thinly sliced
1 bay leaf

'The meat dishes at Avoca always seem so homely and welcoming, as if you are part of the family sitting round for supper'

'Normandy pork is a no-frills, straight-forward interpretation of what is essentially a peasant dish'

Normandy pork

Roast pork and apple sauce may make an ideal Sunday lunch but it is not really suitable for serving in the cafés. Still, the idea appealed to one chef so much that she worked out the following recipe, which has proved equally popular. Quite often dishes emerge from one source and metamorphose into something quite different. Practicality counts for quite a lot and if you look hard enough it is usually possible to trace back a dish's origins.

Toss the pork in the flour. Heat the vegetable oil in a large frying pan, add the meat in small batches and sauté until golden brown, transferring it to a casserole dish. You may need more oil.

Gently sauté the onions and apples in the pan for 10 minutes without colouring. Add to the meat, then pour in the apple juice and stock and season with salt and pepper. Simmer over a low heat for 1 hour or until the meat is tender. Stir in the cream just before serving and adjust the seasoning if necessary.

1.3kg/3lb leg of pork, diced
2 tablespoons plain flour, generously seasoned with salt and pepper
4 tablespoons vegetable oil
2 onions, peeled and chopped
3 cooking apples, peeled, cored and chopped
300ml/$\frac{1}{2}$ pint apple juice
600ml/1 pint chicken or vegetable stock
300ml/$\frac{1}{2}$ pint double cream
Serves 6

Spanish pork

Doreen Fitzmaurice worked in the Basque country in northern Spain during a year out with her children and came back with this recipe, among many others, which reflects the rich culinary tradition of that region.

Toss the pork in the seasoned flour. Heat the vegetable oil in a large frying pan, add the meat in small batches and sauté until golden brown, transferring it to a casserole dish as it is done. You may need more oil.

Add the onions to the pan and sauté for 10 minutes without colouring. Add the wine and simmer for 5 minutes to allow the alcohol to burn off, then stir in the tomatoes. Pour this mixture over the meat and season with salt and pepper. Transfer to an oven pre-heated to 180°C/350°F/gas mark 4 and cook for 1 hour or until the meat is tender. If the sauce is a little thin, take out the meat and keep it warm, then boil the sauce over a moderate heat until reduced and slightly thickened. Return the meat to the pan.

Stir in the olives and sprinkle over the basil just before serving.

1.3kg/3lb leg of pork, diced
2 tablespoons plain flour,
   generously seasoned with salt
   and pepper
4 tablespoons vegetable oil
2 onions, peeled and diced
600ml/1 pint red wine
3 x 400g/14oz cans of chopped
   tomatoes
75g/3oz pitted black olives
A bunch of basil, roughly
   chopped
Serves 6

Lakeshore pork

The name of this dish comes from Lakeshore mustard, a wholegrain mustard manufactured in County Tipperary, although you can use any wholegrain mustard if Lakeshore is difficult to obtain. The recipe is adapted from one cooked by Yvonne Dixon, Leylie's mother.

Toss the pork in the seasoned flour and then brown it in some olive oil in small batches. Place in a flameproof casserole dish and cover with the apple juice and stock. Add the mustard and bring to the boil, then transfer to an oven preheated to 180°C/350°F/gas mark 4 for 40 minutes. Remove from the oven, stir in the cream and return to the oven for 10 minutes.

If the sauce is a little thin, remove the meat and keep warm. Put the casserole over a moderate heat and simmer until the sauce is reduced and thickened. Return the meat to the pan.

1.3kg/3lb diced leg of pork, well trimmed (fillet is even better)
Seasoned flour: flour, salt, pepper, mustard powder and brown sugar
olive oil
600ml/1 pint apple juice
300ml/½ pint chicken stock
2 tablespoons Lakeshore mustard, or other wholegrain mustard
300ml/½ pint cream

VEGETABLE MAIN COURSES

'When vegetables are prepared as they are here I want for nothing else; robust flavours and brilliant colours – paradise'

Piperade tartlets, page 118

Vegetables form the core of what we do in the cafés, alongside the salads, with a great many customers opting for a meat-free meal without realising it. This runs very much in line with the general trend away from the tradition of meat and two vegetables which used to be so prevalent throughout the country.

But perhaps it can also be accounted for by the change in what we eat. Gone are the days when vegetables were steamed cabbage and soggy Brussels sprouts. Now you can choose from roasted red peppers and grilled aubergines to steamed root vegetables tossed in spiced and herbed butter, from lasagnes and all manner of

pasta dishes to bakes, gratins, stews and casseroles that take their inspiration from China and Japan, Italy and Spain, South America and Australia.

It is no accident that we use whole boxes of red and yellow peppers, inky-black aubergines and lush, green courgettes. Like, seemingly, the rest of the world, we have taken Italy to our hearts and why not? This is a country that does really understand vegetables. The Italian obsession with herbs, too, has rubbed off on us and herbs are now a hallmark of many of the dishes served in the cafés.

Our celebration of all things Italian is not to

Ricotta and sweetcorn roulade, page 117

the detriment of our own cuisine, however, and the Irish fondness for root vegetables is still apparent in dishes such as the potato and celeriac gratin on page 101, as well as our enthusiasm for savoury tarts and quiches, both extremely well suited to a café environment.

If you are lucky enough to have your own garden, sourcing vegetables will hardly be a hardship. For most of us, however, the dearth of greengrocers means the supermarket or corner shop. For all the criticism levelled against the large chains, they have brought good-quality vegetables, from humble roots to the more exotic, within our grasp. Don't be slavish, however; if what you want is not up to scratch, seek out an alternative and be prepared to cook something else. Wizened vegetables are good for no one.

Seasonality helps here – don't go searching for asparagus in winter, parsnips in summer or peppers when there is frost on the ground. That said, many vegetables have become year round with the advent of poly tunnels and imports. But who wants everything all the time? With vegetables particularly, there is every reason to celebrate the changing seasons as and when nature dictates, rather than when we pine for a change.

Potato and celeriac gratin

This makes a good accompaniment to lamb, either in early spring, when the weather is still quite chilly, or in autumn, as evenings start to close in. In the cafés, however, it is often served with a few salads for a substantial meal.

Grease a large lasagne-type dish with a little of the butter. Arrange a layer of sliced potatoes over the base of the dish and then a layer of sliced celeriac. Repeat until both are used up, finishing with a layer of potato.

Mix the milk, cream, garlic and horseradish sauce together, season well and pour over the potatoes and celeriac. Dot with the remaining butter and cook in an oven preheated to 200°C/400°F/ gas mark 6 for 1 hour or until the vegetables are tender.

75g/3oz butter

1.3kg/3lb potatoes, peeled and
 thinly sliced

600g/1 $\frac{1}{4}$ lb celeriac, peeled and
 thinly sliced

900ml/1 $\frac{1}{2}$ pints full-cream milk

600ml/1 pint double cream

3 garlic cloves, peeled and finely
 chopped

3 tablespoons horseradish sauce

Leek, blue cheese and rocket frittata

Sweat the leeks in the butter until soft. Lightly whisk the eggs together, then mix in the rocket, cooked leeks and some salt and pepper. Heat a 30cm/12 inch lightly oiled ovenproof frying pan and add the egg mixture. Cook on a medium heat, loosening the mixture from the sides of the pan, until set around the edge. Scatter the blue cheese on top and transfer to an oven preheated to 150°C/300°F/gas mark 2 for about 10–15 minutes, until firm.

4 leeks, sliced
25g/1oz butter
15 eggs
A handful of rocket
Olive oil
75g/3oz blue cheese,
  such as Cashel Blue,
  diced or crumbled
Serves 8

Spinach omelette

Pick and wash the spinach; if it is very fresh, blanch until it goes limp. Press it dry, leave to cool and then chop.

Lightly beat the eggs with salt and pepper and stir in the spinach and nuts. Heat the oil in a pan. Add the egg and spinach mixture.

When the omelette is firm place a lid or plate on top and invert. Slide it back to cook on the other side. Remove from the pan by inverting on to a plate.

500g/1lb leaf spinach,
  fresh/frozen
5 eggs
2 tablespoons toasted
  pine nuts (optional)
2 tablespoons olive oil
Serves 2

Spanish omelette

The ultimate convenience food, a perfect snack, store cupboard food of the best kind? The omelette or frittata is so old it has probably come back into fashion several times over. The difference between the two? Not a great deal – the main distinction of the frittata is that it is cooked more slowly. After that it is up to you what goes in, but don't overdo it. Too many ingredients, like too many cooks, spoil the pot.

Heat the olive oil in a large, heavy-based non-stick frying pan, add the diced potatoes, then season and cook, covered, until the potatoes are cooked but still slightly firm. Do not allow them to colour. Then add the onion and fry until soft. Whisk the eggs with some salt and pepper, pour them into the pan and cook over a low heat until the egg sets without colouring too much underneath. Place a lid or a large plate on top of the frying pan and invert. Then slide the omelette back into the pan on the uncooked side. Tidy the edges to make it rounded and cook until set underneath. Don't overcook, as traditionally the centre should remain moist and soft. Turn out on to a plate and serve warm.

6 tablespoons olive oil
900g/2lb potatoes, peeled and
    cut into small dice
1 large onion, peeled and
    coarsely chopped or sliced
15 eggs
Serves 8

Variations

Smoked salmon: omit the onion and add 110g/4oz smoked salmon, cut into strips, 110g/4oz cream cheese and 1 tablespoon chopped fresh dill. Add after the eggs, so the salmon and dill float on the top.

Cherry tomato, rosemary and goat's cheese: once the egg mixture has set underneath, add 10 cherry tomatoes, halved, 10 semi sun-dried tomatoes, 110g/4oz goat's cheese, crumbled, and 1 dessertspoon chopped fresh rosemary.

Sun-dried tomato, olive and ricotta stuffed baked potatoes

The variations on this simple midweek supper dish are endless. Be sure to choose good spuds: watery ones will never do. Use these suggestions as a basis for experimentation. Most recipes are there to be adapted – we do it all the time!

Prick the potatoes, rub the skins with vegetable oil and then with salt and bake in an oven preheated to 180°C/350°F/gas mark 4 for 1 hour or until tender. Remove from the oven, slice the top off each potato and discard. Scoop out the potato flesh and mash in a bowl with the ricotta and some salt and pepper. Stir in the tomatoes, olives and basil. Refill the potato skins generously – it doesn't matter if they start to overflow – and top with the Gruyère. Reheat the potatoes in the oven until the cheese has just melted and the filling is warmed through.

4 large baking potatoes
A little vegetable oil
110g/4oz ricotta cheese
50g/2oz semi sun-dried
  tomatoes, roughly chopped
10 pitted black olives, roughly
  chopped
A bunch of basil, roughly
  chopped
2 tablespoons grated Gruyère
  cheese

Variations
Spring onions, blue cheese and parsley; Crème fraîche, chives and pine nuts; Grated Cheddar and chutney; Garlic butter and finely chopped thyme.

Mediterranean lasagne

Lightly coat the vegetables in olive oil, spread them on a baking sheet and bake in an oven preheated to 180°C/350°F/gas mark 4 until tender. The aubergines and onions will take about 20 minutes, the peppers 15 minutes and the courgettes 10 minutes. Remove from the oven and leave to cool, then mix with the tomato sauce and season with salt and pepper. Stir in the basil leaves.

Lightly oil a large shallow ovenproof dish, or smaller individual dishes. Pour in a layer of white sauce then add a layer of pasta, then the vegetable mixture, then another layer of pasta, then more vegetable mixture and a final layer of pasta, finishing with white sauce. Bake at 180°C/350°F/gas mark 4 for 35–40 minutes or until brown and bubbling. Sprinkle over the Parmesan and serve.

350g/12oz aubergines, roughly chopped

2 red onions, peeled and quartered

450g/1lb red and yellow peppers, chopped

350g/12oz courgettes, roughly chopped

Olive oil

1 quantity of tomato sauce (see page 184)

A bunch of basil

1 quantity of white sauce (see page 184)

225g/8oz no-need-to-precook lasagne

4 tablespoons freshly grated Parmesan cheese

Lentil and nut loaf

The combination of lentils and nuts may sound quite dated (let's face it, nothing could be more quintessentially Seventies), yet it remains as popular as ever. From the era that gave us flares, sandals and tie-dye comes the everlasting culinary wonder: vegetarian food that appeals to non-vegetarians.

Line the base and sides of a 900g/2lb loaf tin with baking parchment. Place the Puy and orange lentils in separate pans, cover each with cold water and cook until they begin to split – approximately 12–14 minutes for the Puy lentils, 8 minutes for the orange lentils. Drain and place in a mixing bowl.

Melt the butter in a large saucepan and add all the diced vegetables, garlic, chilli and cumin. Cook over a low heat for about 5 minutes, being careful not to overcook the mixture or the vegetables will lose their colour. Remove from the heat and add to the lentils with the breadcrumbs, cheese, nuts and eggs. Mix thoroughly, then season well and taste. The mixture should be quite highly seasoned but not too salty. Place in the lined loaf tin and bake in an oven preheated to 170°C/325°F/gas mark 3 for 45 minutes, until firm to the touch. Turn out and cut into slices to serve. It can be eaten hot or cold. Chutney makes a good accompaniment.

50g/2oz Puy lentils

300g/11oz orange lentils

50g/2oz butter

1 large onion, peeled and
  chopped

3 carrots, peeled and diced

1 large red pepper, diced

3 celery sticks, diced

6 garlic cloves, peeled and
  crushed

$\frac{1}{2}$ fresh red chilli, deseeded and
  finely chopped

2 heaped teaspoons ground
  cumin

75g/3oz fresh breadcrumbs

150g/5oz Cheddar cheese,
  grated

75g/3oz roasted nuts, such as
  pistachios, hazelnuts, peanuts,
  chopped

6 eggs

The Avoca mill in Avoca village

Spinach, roast pepper and tomato roulade

In all the cafés the food is arranged in chill cabinets so that customers can see what they are ordering. Colour, therefore, plays a vital role; if everything is red it shows up rather glaringly. This green and red roulade is just one example of the importance of colour contrast when creating dishes.

Line a 30 x 23cm/12 x 9 inch swiss roll tin with foil and grease lightly. Wash the spinach well, removing the stalks, then put it in a pan with just the water clinging to its leaves and cook for about 2 minutes, until it begins to wilt. Remove from the heat immediately, drain well and chop finely. Melt the butter over a very low heat, add the onion and cook until translucent. Then add the flour and cook, stirring, for 2 minutes. Gradually stir in the milk, increase the heat slightly and cook, stirring continuously, until the mixture is very thick. Remove from the heat, stir in the spinach, egg yolks and cheese and season with salt, pepper and nutmeg. Transfer to a large bowl.

Whisk the egg whites with a pinch of salt until they form stiff peaks and stir into the spinach mixture. Pour into the prepared tin, sprinkle with sesame seeds and bake in an oven preheated to 200°C/400°F/gas mark 6 for 10 minutes, until risen and just firm to the touch.

To make the filling, gently sauté the onion in the olive oil for 10 minutes without colouring. Add the garlic, chilli and roasted peppers and cook for 2 minutes. Add the tomatoes and cook, uncovered, until the mixture has reduced in volume by half. Season to taste and leave to cool slightly.

To assemble, turn the roulade out on to a piece of foil and then peel off the backing foil. Spread the red pepper mixture over the roulade, roll up (see the photograph on page 117) and slice. Serve warm.

110g/4oz fresh spinach
40g/1 ½oz butter
50g/2oz onion, peeled and
   finely chopped
40g/1 ½oz plain flour
300ml/½ pint milk
4 eggs, separated
40g/1 ½oz Parmesan cheese,
   freshly grated
Freshly grated nutmeg
Sesame seeds
For the filling
110g/4oz onion, peeled and
   chopped
2 tablespoons olive oil
2 garlic cloves, peeled and
   crushed
½ fresh red chilli, deseeded and
   finely chopped
2 red peppers, roasted
   (see page 185) and diced
400g/14oz can of tomatoes

Ricotta and sweetcorn roulade

Roulades are consistently popular and are attractive and easy to serve for a buffet lunch. Rolling them up can seem somewhat daunting the first time but it is really very straightforward.

Line a 36 x 26cm/14$\frac{1}{2}$ x 10$\frac{1}{2}$ inch swiss roll tin with baking parchment. Melt 25g/1oz of the butter in a pan, add the leeks, then cover and sweat until soft. Add the garlic, cook for 1 minute, then remove from the heat and set aside.

In a separate pan melt the remaining butter over a low heat, add the flour and cook, stirring, for 5 minutes. Remove from the heat and gradually whisk in the milk. Stir over a medium heat until the mixture boils and thickens; it should be fairly thick. Stir in the egg yolks, leek mixture and 4 tablespoons of the grated Parmesan and transfer to a large bowl.

Whisk the egg whites with a good pinch of salt until they form stiff peaks. Gently fold them into the leek mixture and spread evenly in the swiss roll tin. Bake in an oven preheated to 200°C/400°F/gas mark 6 for 15 minutes or until firm to the touch in the middle.

Allow the roulade to cool slightly, then turn it out on to a sheet of aluminium foil that has been sprinkled with the remaining grated Parmesan. Mix together all the ingredients for the filling and season to taste. Spread the filling evenly over the roulade and roll up (see picture on the right). Serve at room temperature.

110g/4oz butter
4 medium leeks, sliced
2 garlic cloves, crushed
40g/1$\frac{1}{2}$oz plain flour
300ml/$\frac{1}{2}$ pint milk
4 eggs, separated
6 tablespoons freshly grated
   Parmesan cheese
For the filling
225g/8oz ricotta or cottage
   cheese
400g/14oz can of sweetcorn,
   drained and rinsed
2 tablespoons chopped fresh
   chives

'Vegetables used to mean meat and two veg in Ireland...now it's often three veg and skip the meat. But then our treatment of vegetables has moved on somewhat'

Piperade tartlets

Take care when buying the peppers, avoiding any that look washed out and watery. You need good colour and depth, otherwise they tend to taste of little and dissolve when cooked. The same can be said of the tomatoes: buy as well as you can, the essence of this dish is in the vegetables.

Roll the pastry out and use to line four 10cm/4 inch loose-bottomed tartlet tins, then bake blind (see page 186). To make the piperade, heat half the olive oil in a saucepan, add the onion and peppers and cook over a high heat for about 10 minutes, stirring. Turn the heat down and cook for about an hour, until the mixture resembles marmalade.

Slice the goat's cheese and crumble it over the pastry bases. Spread the piperade over it, then arrange the tomatoes on top. Bake in an oven preheated to 200°C/400°F/gas mark 6 for about 20 minutes. Tear up the basil and mix with the remaining olive oil. Spread over the top of the tartlets and serve warm.

1 quantity of shortcrust pastry (see page 186)
4 tablespoons olive oil
1 onion, peeled, cut in half, then sliced into semi-circles
3 red and 3 yellow peppers, cut into strips
225g/8oz goat's cheese log, such as Saint Loup
4 beef or plum tomatoes, sliced
A large bunch of basil

Spinach, pecan and blue cheese pies

Part of the culinary revolution in Ireland over recent years has been the emergence of farmhouse cheesemakers. This dish incorporates Cashel Blue, made in the centre of the country near the wonderful Rock of Cashel. It has a smooth, rounded but tangy flavour and is very good to cook with.
If you want to serve this as a starter, use Yorkshire pudding tins or muffin tins to make individual pies.

Layer the filo into individual Yorkshire pie or muffin tins as shown opposite, brushing each layer with melted butter as you go. Allow the edges of the pastry to hang out over the side of the tins; it will look a bit of a mess at this stage.

Mix together the spinach, pecan nuts, blue cheese and cranberries, if using. Season with salt and pepper and place in the filo pastry shells. Whisk together the eggs and egg yolks, crème fraîche, nutmeg to taste and a seasoning of salt and pepper. Pour over the other ingredients and bake in an oven preheated to 180°C/350°F/ gas mark 4 for 20–25 minutes, until the filling is set. Take care, as the filo is delicate and can easily burn towards the end.

8–10 sheets of filo pastry
Melted butter for brushing
700g/1 $\frac{1}{2}$ lb baby spinach leaves, shredded
4 tablespoons pecan nuts
175g/6oz Cashel Blue or other blue cheese, crumbled
50g/2oz cranberries (optional)
2 eggs plus 3 egg yolks
4 tablespoons crème fraîche
Freshly grated nutmeg

Asparagus, smoked bacon and Gruyère quiche

This is a perfect early-summer dish to make when the short asparagus season starts and you are not too sure just what the weather is doing. Try to get dry-cure bacon, which leaches less water and has a better flavour.

Roll out the pastry and use to line a 28cm/11 inch loose-bottomed flan tin, then bake blind (see page 186).

Fry the bacon in its own fat until crisp, then set aside. Heat the butter in a pan, add the leeks and cook gently for 5 minutes. Blanch the asparagus in a large pan of boiling salted water, then drain well, refresh in cold water and drain again.

Whisk the eggs and egg yolks with the cream and some salt and pepper. Place the leeks, bacon and Gruyère in the pastry shell, then pour the egg mixture over them. Strategically place the asparagus spears in a wheel-type design on top. Bake in an oven preheated to 180°C/350°F/gas mark 4 for 40 minutes or until set and lightly coloured.

1 quantity of shortcrust pastry (see page 186)
225g/8oz smoked bacon lardons
50g/2oz butter
350g/12oz leeks, thinly sliced
16 asparagus spears, trimmed
4 eggs and 5 egg yolks, mixed together
900ml/1 $\frac{1}{2}$ pints double cream
175g/6oz Gruyère cheese, grated

BREADS

'The Avoca brown bread has all you could want in a loaf: moist, full of flavour and with a real zing and bite to it, just as bread used to be'

Multiseed brown, page 132

Ireland has gone through a sea-change in its attitude to bread over the last 25 years: from basic soda bread baked in domestic kitchens to the ubiquitous sliced white to par-baked French bread, and round once again to home-baked soda bread, now supplemented by the likes of focaccia, multiseed, black olive and sun-dried tomato bread.

When Avoca started baking bread it was one of the few establishments apart from the most expensive restaurants to do so. Our brown bread recipe has been asked for more times than anyone can remember, so often that it was eventually printed on a postcard.

As Simon Pratt points out, so much bread is baked too quickly, goes stale rapidly and tastes of nothing. "Biased as I am," he says honestly, "the multiseed bread, toasted even four days after it was made, still makes the best toast in the world."

There is such a demand for Avoca bread, both in the cafés and to take away, that a separate bakery was built at Kilmacanogue a few years ago. This is run by second-generation baker Danny Smith, who comments that his father would be amazed at how much labour modern equipment replaces. "When I said I wanted to bake, he did everything he could to dissuade

Ciabatta rolls, page 137

me," Danny says, grinning. "But it is nothing like as physically demanding as when I was young." No surprise, then, to find his own son, also called Danny, following in his father's footsteps. Danny's favourite breads are the Avoca brown bread, a a cheesy white yeast bread and his white and brown soda breads. During a busy day he can bake up to 400 loaves and 400 scones, which may seem a lot but, as he points out, he baked at least as many with his father but much of the mixing was done by hand. "It's still physically exhausting but as satisfying as ever. I baked my first loaf in my mother's kitchen aged ten and I enjoy it as much today as I did then."

There is no secret to bread baking, but it does take practice. Although only using three ingredients, flour, yeast and water, there is an incredible variation in how they behave depending on location, who is baking, and what your oven is like. Even the water can vary, from hard to soft and in its mineral content.

There is a final ingredient and that is time. Good bread requires space to develop its flavour and character, you cannot rush a good loaf. Take time to experiment with different flours, they vary enormously and behave very differently depending on the weather and indeed, your mood and the more exciting ones require searching out.

White yeast bread

Plain and traditional, good white bread is everywhere now, whereas a few years ago it was hard to find anything other than sliced white. Bread says a great deal about culture – look at France – and the enormous improvement in the quality and variety of Irish bread is just one indicator of the emerging modern Ireland.

Dissolve the yeast in 150ml/¼ pint of lukewarm water. Put the butter and sugar into a bowl with 150ml/¼ pint of very hot water and stir until the sugar has dissolved and the butter has melted, then add 150ml/¼ pint of cold water. By now the liquid should be lukewarm, or blood heat, so combine it with the yeast mixture.

Sift the flour and salt into a bowl, make a well in the centre and pour in most of the lukewarm liquid. Mix to a loose dough, adding the remaining liquid; add more flour or more water, too, if necessary. Turn the dough out on to a floured board, cover and leave to relax for 5–10 minutes. Then knead for 10 minutes or until smooth and springy (if kneading in a food mixer with a dough hook, 5 minutes is usually long enough). Put the dough in a bowl and cover tightly with clingfilm, then leave in a warm place until doubled in size – the rising time will depend on the temperature.

Knock back the risen dough and knead for 2–3 minutes, until all the air has been forced out again. Leave to relax for 10 minutes, then shape into loaves, plaits or rolls. Place loaves in two 450g/1lb baking tins that have been brushed with olive oil, or plaits or rolls on an oiled baking sheet. Cover with a light tea towel and leave to rise again in a warm place; this rising will be much shorter, only about 20–30 minutes. It is ready for baking if a small dent remains when the dough is pressed lightly with your finger. Brush with the egg glaze and sprinkle with poppy or sesame seeds, if using. Bake in an oven preheated to 230°C/450°F/gas mark 8 for 30–35 minutes, until the loaves have risen, are golden brown and sound hollow when tapped underneath. Leave on a rack to cool.

20g/¾oz fresh yeast
25g/1oz butter
15g/½oz granulated sugar
700g/1½lb strong white flour
2 teaspoons salt
1 egg beaten with 1 tablespoon water (or 1 egg yolk beaten with 2 tablespoons cream), to glaze
Poppy seeds or sesame seeds for topping (optional)

Brown bread

It is so easy these days to forget how basic bread is. Eat a piece of this brown bread and you realise it is real food, not something manufactured and totally devoid of flavour. With a bowl of soup it is a true feast: the best ingredients, handled simply.

Mix all the dry ingredients together in a large bowl. Add the treacle and stir in enough of the milk to give a moist but not sloppy mixture. Place in a well-oiled loaf tin 900g/2lb loaf tin and bake in an oven preheated to 200°C/400°F/gas mark 6 for 20 minutes or until risen. Reduce the heat to 170°C/325°F/gas mark 3 and bake for a further hour.

Run a knife around the tin and ease the bread out. If it sounds hollow when tapped on the bottom it is cooked; if not, return it to the oven for 10–15 minutes. There is no need to put the bread back in the tin; turn it upside down and put it directly on the shelf.

200g/6oz white flour
300g/11oz coarse brown
  flour
3 tablespoons of bran
2 tablespoons of wheatgerm
2 heaped teaspoons baking
  powder
1 level teaspoon salt
1 dessertspoon treacle
600–900ml/1–1 ½ pints
  milk
Makes 1 loaf

¼ Cup milk)
1½ T molasses
2 T light corn
    syrup

Soda bread

This is the bread baked in countless cottages around Ireland. Simple and cheap to make, with easily obtainable ingredients, it fed hungry farmers and their families for years. Today it is as popular as ever, its honest simplicity appealing in an age when food seems to get ever more complicated.

Mix all the dry ingredients together in a large bowl. Gradually mix in the buttermilk to give a moist dough. Place in a greased 900g/2lb loaf tin and bake in an oven preheated to 230°C/450°F/gas mark 8 for 30 minutes, until the loaf sounds hollow when turned out of the tin and tapped underneath. Place on a wire rack to cool.

450g/1lb plain flour
1 level teaspoon bicarbonate of soda
1 teaspoon caster sugar
$\frac{1}{2}$ teaspoon salt
About 400ml/14fl oz buttermilk
Makes 1 large loaf

Fruit soda

Fruit soda is one of the simplest breads to make. You can even have it ready on the breakfast table if you are an early riser.

Mix all the dry ingredients together in a bowl. Then slowly add the buttermilk and mix well to form a dough. Shape it into a mound, place in a greased 900g/2lb loaf tin and bake for 20 minutes in an oven preheated to 190°C/375°F/gas mark 5. Lower the heat to 170°C/325°F/gas mark 3 and continue baking for 25 minutes. The loaf should sound hollow when you turn it out of the tin and tap the bottom; if in doubt, turn it upside down and bake for a further 10 minutes. Leave the loaf on a wire rack to cool.

450g/1lb plain flour
1 level teaspoon bicarbonate of soda
25g/1oz caster sugar
A pinch of salt
25g/1oz sultanas
About 400ml/14fl oz buttermilk
Makes 1 large loaf

Multiseed brown bread with fruit

This bread keeps amazingly well and makes great toast, especially when grilled on a ridged grill pan and served with crisp bacon and grilled tomatoes. Butter and jam are good with it, but so too are ham and eggs, smoked salmon and cream cheese, or a few slices of bacon, post pub. The seed content can be altered to provide variety, or to cope with a shortage in your storecupboard.

Mix all the dry ingredients together in a large bowl. Add the treacle and enough milk to make a moist dough, like stiff porridge. Place in a greased 900g/2lb baking tin and bake in an oven preheated to 180°C/350°F/gas mark 4 for 1 hour, or until the loaf is well browned and sounds hollow when turned out of the tin and tapped underneath. Leave on a wire rack to cool.

200g/6oz plain flour
350g/11oz coarse brown flour
50g/2oz bran
25g/1oz wheatgerm
2 heaped teaspoons baking powder
1 level teaspoon salt
1 tablespoon sesame seeds
1 tablespoon poppy seeds
2 tablespoons sunflower seeds
1 tablespoon linseeds
2 tablespoons pumpkin seeds
50g/2oz sultanas
50g/2oz semi-dried apricots, chopped
1 tablespoon treacle
600–900ml/1–1 ½ pints milk
Makes 1 large loaf

'Good bread is one of life's treats, particularly in this age of instant food – a reminder of exactly who and what we really are'

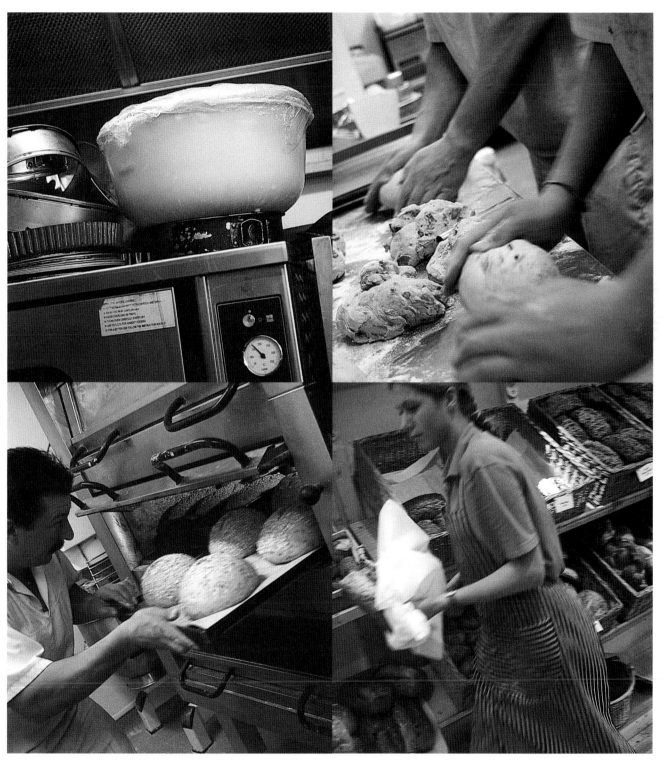

Pictured overleaf: from left granary brown rolls and ciabatta rolls, page 137

Banana bread

The banana lends this bread a moist richness, making it almost like a healthy brioche, or a modern version of a teatime brack. It also makes a rather delicious but rich version of bread and butter pudding.

Sift the flour, salt, baking powder and cinnamon into a bowl and stir in the sugar. Mix in the egg, sunflower oil and vanilla essence but do not beat. Fold in the pecans and mashed bananas, using a fork. Again do not beat. Spoon into a lined 900g/2lb loaf tin and bake in an oven preheated to 180°C/350°F/gas mark 4 for 50–60 minutes, until the loaf is golden brown and springs back when prodded gently with your finger. Leave in the tin for 10 minutes, then turn out on to a wire rack to cool.

225g/8oz plain flour
1 teaspoon salt
1 heaped teaspoon baking
  powder
1 teaspoon ground cinnamon
110g/4oz caster sugar
1 egg, beaten
75ml/3fl oz sunflower oil
A few drops of vanilla essence
65g/2½oz pecan nuts, chopped
4 medium-sized ripe bananas,
  mashed
Makes 1 loaf

'Who would have thought of putting bananas into bread? Not me, but I just want to go on eating it – perfect comfort food'

Avoca scones

Sift the flour, baking powder and salt into a bowl and stir in the sugar. Using your fingertips, lightly work in the butter until the mixture resembles dry breadcrumbs. Add the egg, cream and enough milk to moisten. Mix well until it has a soft, doughy texture – but it shouldn't be too moist.

Gather the dough into a ball and turn it out on to a floured surface, then roll lightly with a rolling pin to 2.5cm/1 inch thick. Cut out with a round cutter, transfer to a greased baking sheet and brush the tops with the egg glaze. Bake in an oven preheated to 180°C/350°F/gas mark 4 for 15–20 minutes or until well browned.

450g/1lb self-raising flour
A pinch of baking powder
A generous pinch of salt
50g/2oz caster sugar
110g/4oz unsalted butter, diced
1 egg, lightly beaten
50ml/2fl oz double cream
200ml/7fl oz milk (you may
   need a little more)
1 egg beaten with 1 tablespoon
   water, to glaze
Makes 12–18

Avoca brown scones

Put the flour, salt and baking powder in a bowl and rub in the butter until the mixture resembles fine breadcrumbs. Make a well in the centre, add the egg and milk and mix well. You may need to add more milk, depending on humidity. Turn the dough on to a floured surface and roll out to 2.5cm/1 inch thick. Cut out with a round cutter and transfer to a greased baking sheet. Brush with the egg glaze, sprinkle with sesame seeds, then bake in an oven preheated to 180°C/350°F/gas mark 4 for 15–20 minutes.

225g/8oz coarse brown flour
225g/8oz plain white flour
A generous pinch of salt
1 heaped teaspoon baking powder
110g/4oz butter
1 egg
300ml/10fl oz milk
1 egg beaten with 1 tablespoon
   water, to glaze
Sesame seeds
Makes 12–18

Apple streusel biscuits

This is an almond shortcake biscuit with a rich streusel topping, a popular teatime treat.

Sift the flour and icing sugar into a bowl and stir in the ground almonds. Rub in the butter until the mixture forms coarse crumbs, then work gently together to form a soft dough. Roll out to fit a 32 x 23cm/13 x 9 inch swiss roll tin. Scoop the dough into the tin and press out to fit. Prick all over with a fork. Spread the lemon curd on top and refrigerate while making the streusel topping.

Coarsely grate the apple and squeeze dry on kitchen paper. Put into a bowl with a little of the demerara sugar and mix to separate the strands. In a separate bowl, rub the butter into the flour until the mixture resembles fine breadcrumbs. Mix in the spice, apple and the remaining sugar. Sprinkle evenly over the lemon curd, pressing down gently. Bake in an oven preheated to 180°C/350°F/gas mark 4 for 45–50 minutes, until lightly browned. Leave to cool in the tin, then cut into bars. Dust with caster sugar.

150g/5oz plain flour
90g/3 ½ oz icing sugar
150g/5oz ground almonds
225g/8oz unsalted butter, diced
6 tablespoons home-made
  lemon curd (see page 179)
A little caster sugar for dusting
For the streusel topping
1 large red eating apple
90g/3 ½ oz demerara sugar
90g/3 ½ oz unsalted butter, diced
190g/6 ½ oz plain flour, sifted
1 teaspoon mixed spice
Makes 16–20

Italian chocolate fridge biscuits

Put the butter, cocoa powder, sugar and ground almonds and ground hazelnuts in a large pan and heat gently, stirring, until the butter has melted. Beat the coffee into the mixture along with the egg and egg yolk, then fold in the biscuits, honeycomb (both of which should be chopped up) and chopped hazelnuts. Lightly oil a shallow 23 x 32cm/9 x 13 inch baking tin and press the mixture into it – you are aiming for a thickness of about 2cm/¾ inch. Leave it in the fridge overnight, then turn out and cut into squares.

175g/6oz unsalted butter
150g/5oz cocoa powder
175g/6oz caster sugar
75g/3oz ground almonds
75g/3oz ground hazelnuts
1 tablespoon strongly brewed
  black coffee
1 egg and 1 egg yolk, lightly
  beaten together
175g/6oz Petit Beurre biscuits
175g/6oz honeycomb
  (we use Crunchie bars)
175g/6oz hazelnuts, finely
  chopped

Bir's biccies (Bakewell biscuits)

Bir worked in the kitchens at Powerscourt until she retired from commercial cooking. She supplied bis-
cuits to Kilmacanogue in the early days and then started cooking full time. These biscuits are essentially
a reworking of Bakewell tart, surely one of the most delicious desserts known to man or woman.

Roll out the pastry and use to line a 38 x 30.5 x 4cm/15 x 12 x
1½ inch deep tin. Thinly cover with raspberry jam. Combine the
butter, rice, ground almonds, sugar, eggs and almond essence. Pour
over the jam, top with flaked almonds and bake in an oven preheated to 180°C/350°F/gas mark 4 for 40–45 minutes. Leave to
cool before cutting into fingers. If you cut this tart while warm it
tends to make a bit of a mess. Better to leave it overnight, or at
least until it comes to room temperature.

Double quantity of shortcrust
   pastry (see page 186)
3 tablespoons home-made
   raspberry jam
500g/1lb 2oz unsalted butter,
   melted and cooled
400g/12oz ground rice
200g/6oz ground almonds
500g/1lb 2oz caster sugar
4 small eggs, lightly whisked
1-2 drops of natural almond
   essence
A few flaked almonds for
   sprinkling

Pictured overleaf, a selection of Avoca biscuits and cookies

Muesli biscuits

Put the melted butter, sugar and golden syrup in a bowl and mix until combined. Mix all the dry ingredients together and beat them into the butter and sugar. Press into a large Swiss roll tin so the mixture is about 2cm/³⁄₄ inch thick and cut out using a biscuit cutter. Bake in an oven preheated to 180°C/350°F/gas mark 4 for 20–25 minutes, until golden brown. Transfer to a wire rack to cool.

450g/1lb unsalted butter, melted and cooled
225g/8oz caster sugar
4 tablespoons golden syrup
225g/8oz plain flour
50g/2oz desiccated coconut
600g/1 ¼ lb oatmeal
A pinch of bicarbonate of soda

'We are a nation of tea drinkers, but a cup of tea is so much better with a little something to nibble on. That it is home made with real butter makes it all the more special'

Chocolate hazelnut cookies

Teatime is a meal all too often overlooked in our modern rush-about life. Being on holiday or out doing a day's shopping or browsing reminds many customers how relaxing it is to take a break. These are Karen Nichols' cookies, one of the most popular teatime treats.

Beat the butter and sugar in a food mixer with the K-beater or paddle attachment until completely combined. Mix in the ground hazelnuts, then the flour and bicarbonate of soda. Finally add the chocolate chips. The dough should stick together. If it is too crumbly, it means the butter was not soft enough, so beat in the mixer for a little longer. If it still does not combine, add 2 tablespoons of milk. Wrap the dough in clingfilm and chill for 1 hour, then roll out on a floured board to 5mm/¼ inch thick. Cut out rounds with a biscuit cutter and place on a baking sheet lined with parchment paper. Bake in an oven preheated to 170°C/325°F/gas mark 3 for 20–25 minutes, until golden brown. Transfer to a wire rack and cool.

300g/11oz butter at room
   temperature
160g/5½oz caster sugar
175g/6oz finely ground
   hazelnuts
600g/1lb 4oz plain flour, sifted
¼ teaspoon bicarbonate
   of soda
450g/1lb chocolate chips
   (dark chocolate tastes best)
*Makes 12–14 very large cookies
or about 25 smaller ones*

Gertie's shortbread

Gertie was essentially a stay-at-home-and-bake mum. For children's parties, everything would be home baked. Even to this day, if you call in for tea, tins of biscuits and cakes will be produced. Old-fashioned baking at its best

Sift the flour, cornflour and icing sugar into a bowl and rub in the butter until the mixture forms a soft ball. Roll out on a lightly floured work surface until it is about 1cm/½ inch thick, then cut out. We use a gingerman cutter and get about 24 men. Place on a baking sheet lined with baking parchment and chill for at least 30 minutes – an hour is better. Bake for 1 hour in an oven preheated to 150°C/300°F/gas mark 2, then transfer to a wire rack and cool.

450g/1lb plain flour
225g/8oz cornflour
225g/8oz icing sugar
450g/1lb unsalted butter,
   diced
Makes about 24

Chocolate orange cake

Break up the chocolate and put it in a bowl set over a pan of simmering water, making sure the water is not touching the base of the bowl. Leave to melt and then remove from the heat and set aside. Beat the butter and sugar together until light and fluffy, then gradually beat in the egg yolks. Stir in the melted chocolate and the orange zest and then fold in the flour. Whisk the egg whites with a pinch of salt until stiff and fold them into the cake mixture. Spoon into a lined round 23cm/9 inch cake tin and bake in an oven preheated to 170°C/325°F/gas mark 3 for 35–40 minutes, until a skewer inserted in the centre comes out clean. Turn out and leave to cool on a wire rack.

To make the icing, put all the ingredients in a bowl set over a pan of simmering water and leave until the chocolate has melted. Stir until smooth, then remove from the heat and set aside for 10–20 minutes. Pour the icing over the cake and decorate with slices of orange.

175g/6oz dark chocolate
  (70 per cent cocoa solids)
175g/6oz unsalted butter
225g/8oz caster sugar
6 eggs, separated
Grated zest of 3 oranges
150g/5oz self-raising flour, sifted
Orange slices, to decorate
For the icing
125ml/4fl oz double cream
225g/8oz dark chocolate
  (55 per cent cocoa solids)
1–2 tablespoons Cointreau

Strawberry meringue roulade

Line a 30 x 20cm/12 x 8 inch swiss roll tin with baking parchment. Put the egg whites and half the caster sugar into a bowl and use an electric whisk to whisk to snowy peaks. Then gradually add the remaining sugar, continuing to whisk for 10–15 minutes, until it forms stiff peaks. Spread the mixture into the tin and bake for 1 hour in an oven preheated to 150°C/300°F/gas mark 2. Remove from the oven and cool. Turn out on to a fresh sheet of baking parchment and carefully peel off the lining paper. Spread over the cream and strawberries and roll up (see photograph on page 117).

4 large egg whites
225g/8oz caster sugar
300ml/½ pint double cream, whipped
450g/1lb strawberries, sliced or quartered
Extra whipped cream and strawberries, to decorate

Chocolate roulade

Line a 28 x 35cm/11 x 14 inch swiss roll tin with foil and grease lightly. Whisk the egg yolks and caster sugar together until the mixture is pale and mousselike and holds a figure of eight when trailed from the whisk. This needs to be done with an electric beater as it is virtually impossible to do by hand. Put the chocolate and water in a bowl set over a pan of simmering water and leave until the chocolate has melted, stirring occasionally until smooth. Leave to cool slightly and then fold into the egg yolk mixture. Whisk the egg whites until they form stiff peaks, then fold them into the chocolate mixture. Pour into the tin and bake in an oven preheated to 180°C/350°F/gas mark 4 for 12–15 minutes, until firm to the touch in the centre. Remove from the oven, cover with a damp tea towel and leave to cool. Turn the roulade out on to a sheet of baking parchment and peel off the foil. Whip the cream and spread it evenly on top, then roll up, using the baking parchment to help (see photograph on page 117). Dust with icing sugar and garnish with chocolate wafers.

5 eggs, separated
175g/6oz caster sugar
175g/6oz dark chocolate
  (55 per cent cocoa solids)
75ml/3fl oz water
300ml/½ pint double cream
Icing sugar and chocolate wafers,
  to decorate
Serves 8–10

Mixed berry tiramisú

Known in the kitchen as posh trifle, this was conceived for an Avoca cookery demonstration on the theme of alternative Christmas dishes.

Put the water and 110g/4oz of the sugar in a large pan and heat gently until dissolved. Bring to the boil and simmer for 2 minutes to make a light syrup. Add the fruit, bring back to the boil and simmer for a further 2 minutes. Strain the fruit, reserving the syrup. Stir the cassis into the syrup. In a large bowl, whisk the egg yolks and the remaining sugar until the mixture is pale and forms ribbons when trailed from the whisk. Whisk in the mascarpone. In a separate bowl, whisk the egg whites with a pinch of salt until they form stiff peaks. Fold them into the mascarpone mixture. Dip half the biscuits into the reserved syrup and use them to line the base of a lasagne-type dish. Spread half the cheese mixture over the biscuits, covering them well. Then spread over half the fruit. Dip the remaining biscuits in the syrup and arrange on top of this fruit mixture, then cover with the remaining fruit. Finally cover everything with the remaining cheese mixture. Cover and chill overnight. Garnish with the toasted flaked almonds and grated chocolate before serving.

150ml/¼ pint water
250g/9oz caster sugar
175g/6oz strawberries
175g/6oz raspberries
175g/6oz blackberries
1 tablespoon crème de cassis
3 eggs, separated
450g/1lb mascarpone cheese
35–40 boudoir or Savoiardi biscuits
50g/2oz toasted flaked almonds
50g/2oz dark chocolate, grated

'I didn't think summer pudding could be bettered until I tried the mixed berry tiramisú – a heavenly concoction of soft fruit and chocolate'

Chocolate and amaretti mousse

Go for a good, strong coffee, otherwise the mousse lacks bite, and don't skimp on the chocolate either. It should have at least 70 per cent cocoa solids for best results.

Put the chocolate, butter, sugar, coffee and brandy in a bowl set over a pan of simmering water, making sure the water is not touching the base of the bowl. While this is melting, lightly crush the amaretti biscuits and sprinkle enough into each ramekin to cover the base, reserving the rest for the top. When the chocolate mixture has melted, stir until smooth and then whisk in the egg yolks. Remove from the heat and fold in the lightly whipped cream. Whisk the egg whites with a pinch of salt until stiff, fold them into the chocolate mixture and pour it over the crushed biscuits. Sprinkle with the remaining amaretti and place in the fridge to set. Serve each portion with a couple of amaretti biscuits on the side.

225g/8oz dark chocolate
110g/4oz unsalted butter
110g/4oz caster sugar
50ml/2fl oz freshly made
    espresso coffee
50ml/2fl oz brandy
30–36 amaretti biscuits,
    plus extra to serve
3 egg yolks
250ml/8fl oz double cream,
    lightly whipped
5 egg whites
Serves 8–12

Pecan and maple tart

Watch out for any dodgy tooth fillings; this is very, very sweet. Americans, however, reckon it is particularly good. Strong coffee is recommended to accompany it, or a nice cup of tea.

Roll out the pastry, use to line a 28cm/11 inch loose-bottomed flan tin, then bake blind (see page 186). To make the filling, put all the ingredients except the pecans in a bowl and beat with a hand whisk until smooth. Sprinkle the pecans over the base of the pastry case and pour in the filling. Place on the middle shelf of an oven pre-heated to 170°C/325°F/gas mark 3 and bake for 1 hour, until set. Remove from the oven and leave to cool on a wire rack.

1 quantity of shortcrust pastry
    (see page 186)
200g/7oz dark soft brown sugar
200ml/7fl oz maple syrup
3 eggs
A pinch of salt
$\frac{1}{2}$ teaspoon vanilla essence
50g/2oz unsalted butter, melted
    and cooled
175g/6oz pecan nuts

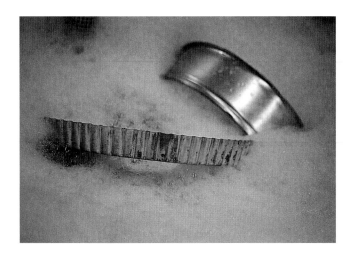

Lemon tart with caramelised strawberries

Writing cookery books using recipes from commercial kitchens means you live, dream and eat a great deal of what you are writing about. About 4pm, when sugar levels are at their lowest and tiredness at its highest I would develop a yearning for Fleur Campbell's lemon tart. Day after day I would eat a spoonful of creamy, lemony delight and then another and another. This is the recipe.

Roll out the pastry, use to line a 28cm/11 inch loose-bottomed flan tin and bake blind (see page 186). Put the sugar and lemon juice in a large bowl and stir until the sugar has dissolved. Add the lemon zest, whisk in the eggs and finally stir in the cream. For best results, leave the filling overnight in the fridge, then remove and stir gently to combine it again. If you don't leave it overnight it will separate during cooking, giving a custard bottom and foamy top. Pour the filling into the baked pastry case and cook in a preheated oven 140°C/275°F/gas mark 1 for 1 hour, until set. Remove from the oven and leave to cool.

To make the caramel, put the sugar and water in a saucepan and heat gently until the sugar has dissolved. Increase the heat and boil until it has changed colour to a light caramel. Dip the strawberries in one at a time, holding them on a fork, and place on an oiled baking sheet to cool. To serve, dust the tart thickly with icing sugar and then caramelise it, if liked, under a very hot grill or with a cook's blowtorch. Decorate with the caramelised strawberries.

1 quantity of shortcrust pastry
  (see page 186)
400g/14oz caster sugar
Juice of 5 lemons
Grated zest of 3 lemons
8 eggs
350ml/12fl oz double cream,
  whipped
Icing sugar for dusting
For the caramelised strawberries
225g/8oz caster sugar
4 tablespoons water
8 large strawberries

Caramelised rhubarb and custard tart

This is a variation on the classic French apple version, which Fleur says is better because the rhubarb is sharper. It is also more consistent, she says, given the inconsistency in apples: you just cannot get them like you used to.

Roll out the pastry, use to line a 28cm/11 inch loose-bottomed flan tin and bake blind (see page 186). Chop, wash and simmer the rhubarb in a covered saucepan over a moderate heat until tender (this can be done the day before).

Combine the rhubarb and custard and pour into the cooked pastry case and bake at 150°C/300°F/gas mark 2. This should just set the custard – if the oven is too hot the tart will end up like scrambled eggs. Cooking time is 45 minutes–1 hour, until it no longer looks like liquid but wobbles when shaken.

Dust the top with caster sugar and caramelise by either using a grill or a cook's blowtorch.

1 quantity of shortcrust pastry
   (see page 186)
700g/1 ½ lb rhubarb
½ quantity of the custard recipe
   (below)
caster sugar

Custard

Put 450ml/¾ pint full-cream milk and a split vanilla pod in a pan and bring to the boil. Remove from the heat and set aside to infuse. Whisk 110g/4oz caster sugar and 5 egg yolks together until pale, then whisk in 2 level tablespoons plain flour. Remove the vanilla pod from the milk and gradually whisk the warm milk into the egg yolk mixture. Pour it into a saucepan and cook, stirring, until it just comes to the boil, then simmer very gently for 2–3 minutes to cook out the floury taste. Whisk in 1 teaspoon of soft butter.

Chocolate and raspberry tart

If you are a confirmed chocoholic it's a good idea to marry somebody who is equally enthusiastic. So it was with Mark Nichols, whose wife Karen invented this tart for his fortieth birthday. The combination is a classic, this rendition particularly good.

Roll out the pastry, use to line a 28cm/11 inch loose-bottomed flan tin and bake blind (see page 186). Remove from the oven and leave to cool. Cover the pastry base with the raspberries. Put the cream and sugar in a large pan and bring to the boil, then remove from the heat and whisk in the chocolate so that it melts. Add the rum. Leave to cool a little, then pour the mixture over the raspberries. Leave in the fridge for 1–2 hours. Decorate with a few more raspberries and serve.

1 quantity of shortcrust pastry
  (see page 186)
375g/13oz fresh raspberries
700ml/24fl oz double cream
25g/1oz caster sugar
500g/18oz dark chocolate
  (the best couverture, if
  possible; otherwise 55–70
  per cent cocoa solids), grated
2 tablespoons rum
Raspberries to decorate

RELISHES

'Home-made chutneys and relishes are a whole different concept when compared to the mass-produced alternatives'

Wicklow raspberry jam, page 174

What comes out of jars depends entirely on what goes into them. Where possible, we do not use preservatives other than sugar and vinegar at Avoca, preferring to allow the natural flavour of the fruit and vegetables to come through. Eat cucumber pickle and it should taste of cucumber; grapefruit marmalade of grapefruit. Ensuring this happens means we tend to rely on small, owner-run companies to supply any preserves we do not make ourselves.

We want customers to be as enthusiastic about the jam as they are about the scone they are spreading it on. Two husband and wife teams, Sara and Philip Moss and Judy and Richard Baker supply us with preserves as diverse as aubergine pickle and rhubarb and ginger jam. They, too, insist on avoiding preservatives and the operations remain small. Although fitted out to gleaming-clean European specifications, they remain essentially cottage industries, following old recipes and employing local people to prepare the various jams and pickles.

There is no need for jam to be smothered in E-numbers – putting fruit and vegetables into jars is one of the oldest preserving processes. Yet overkill can turn the excellent into the insipid. "All the time," says Philip Moss, "we are looking

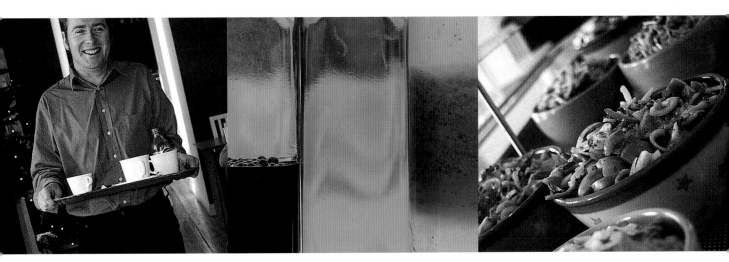

Oils and vinegars, page 181

at how best to make the fruit or vegetables shine. The acidity or sweetness, the spices or flavouring, must work in tandem with that to create some sort of whole, otherwise all you have is pulp and flavouring." Oddly enough, this is exactly what mass-produced jars contain, hence our enthusiasm for using small producers.

When preparing preserves at home you need to maintain a strict standard of hygiene. Contamination can come from the tiniest of errors, dirty tea towels being one of the most common. Ensure that everything is as clean as possible. As with pudding recipes, quantities are important. These are not just guides but should be followed exactly. Leave variations until you are happy with the basic recipe.

All preserves should be stored in sterilised jars. To sterilise jars, you can run them through a dishwasher cycle, which is a great deal easier and just as effective as messing about with boiling water, although the latter is necessary if you don't have a dishwasher. In this case you should submerge the jars in boiling water for 5 minutes, then drain them thoroughly, handling them with a clean tea towel. Finally dry the jars off for 30 minutes or so in a low oven, again taking care to use a clean towel when handling the jars.

Pink grapefruit marmalade

There is no better way to wake up in the morning than to a breakfast of coffee, this marmalade and Avoca brown bread, according to Hilary Pratt. "It's not just the flavour but the colour, too, which seems so appealing," she says. Like all good marmalade it has a delicious, tangy, wake-up quality.

Wash the grapefruit and lemons, peel off the zest thinly with a potato peeler and cut it into slices. Remove the pith from the flesh and cut up the pith roughly. Chop the flesh, reserving the pips and any juice that appears.

Tie the pips and pith in a piece of muslin. Put the zest, flesh, any reserved juice, and the muslin bag in a large saucepan or a preserving pan with the water, bring to the boil and simmer gently for 2 hours, or until the zest is tender and the liquid reduced by half. Remove the muslin, squeezing to extract the juice, and discard.

Warm the sugar in a low oven and add to the mixture. Stir over a low heat until dissolved, then bring to boiling point and simmer until setting point is reached (see Seville orange marmalade on page 172). Remove from the heat and leave to settle for 15 minutes, skimming off any scum that rises to the surface. Pot in hot sterilised jars and seal tightly.

2 large pink grapefruit
450g/1lb lemons
2.25 litres/4 pints water
1.3kg/3lb granulated sugar

'The Avoca jams and preserves
make the most fantastic presents.
Every time I give them away people
want to know where to get more,
they are so fruit driven and fresh'

Seville orange marmalade

Classic, traditional and never bettered. All the cafés have their regular breakfast customers, some businessmen, others just groups that seem to meet regularly. They sometimes hesitate at the counter but inevitably go for our full Avoca breakfast: scones, marmalade, tea or coffee; a quiet corner and the paper or a bit of chat. What better way is there to start the day?

Wash the oranges and lemons, squeeze out the juice, reserving the pips, and then chop the skin; the size depends on what texture you want the marmalade to be. Put the fruit juice, water and chopped skin in a large saucepan or a preserving pan. Tie the pips in a piece of muslin and suspend them in the liquid. Bring to the boil and simmer for 2 hours or until the peel is tender. Meanwhile, put the sugar to warm in a low oven. Remove the muslin bag, squeezing out as much of the liquid as possible. Add the sugar to the pan and cook over a low heat until it has dissolved. Turn up the heat and boil rapidly until setting point is reached. To test this, put a little marmalade on a cold saucer from the fridge for a few minutes. Push the marmalade with your finger; if it wrinkles it is set. Remove the pan from the heat, allow the marmalade to settle for 15 minutes and then transfer to hot sterilised jars and seal.

1.5kg/3½lb Seville oranges
2 lemons
3.6 litres/6 pints water
2.6kg/6lb granulated sugar

Rhubarb and ginger jam

A little spicy for breakfast, perhaps, but perfect for afternoon tea, when a kick of sugar and spice is just what is needed. Spread on some Avoca scones (see page 143) along with plenty of butter and worry about the calories tomorrow; everyone should have afternoon tea once in a while.

Wipe the rhubarb and cut it into 2.5cm/1 inch pieces. Layer it with the sugar in a large bowl. Add the lemon juice and zest, then cover and leave to stand overnight. The next day, put the mixture in a pre-serving pan, add the fresh ginger tied in a piece of muslin and simmer until the mixture becomes a thick pulp. Test for setting point (see Seville orange marmalade on page 172). When this is reached, remove from the heat and stir in the stem ginger. Discard the muslin bag. Pot the jam in hot sterilised jars and seal tightly.

1.8kg/4lb trimmed rhubarb
1.8kg/4lb granulated sugar
Juice and zest of 2 lemons
50g/2oz fresh ginger, bruised
50g/2oz stem ginger in syrup,
    drained and chopped

Wicklow raspberry jam

So called because in the early days we were able to source all the raspberries from Wicklow. These days, however, demand has far outstripped supply from this beautiful county and we have to source further afield. The recipe remains the same, however.

Put the raspberries into a large saucepan or a preserving pan over a low heat and cook slowly, stirring very gently so as not to break up the fruit. As the juices start to run, fold the top fruit in, then allow to cook for 30 minutes or until the raspberries are very soft. Meanwhile, put the sugar in a bowl in a low oven to warm through. Stir the sugar into the fruit and cook gently for 15 minutes, until the sugar has dissolved. Turn the heat right up and boil rapidly for 10 minutes or until setting point is reached (see Seville orange marmalade on page 172). Remove the pan from the heat, let the jam settle for 15 minutes, then skim off any scum from the surface. Pot in hot sterilised jars and seal tightly.

1.8kg/4lb raspberries
1.8kg/4lb granulated sugar

Pictured overleaf: Apple chutney, page 178, with granary bread and Gubeen cheese

Apple chutney

This is one of our best-selling chutneys, a perfect partner for cheese and a delight with cold meats. It is crucial to use a good vinegar, too often chutney is let down by this vital ingredient, it should play an integral, supporting role and not dominate. After all, you want the fruit to shine, to taste the bright apple flavour, not end up wincing at the acidity

Put all the ingredients in a large saucepan and simmer over a moderate heat until tender and slightly thickened. Pot in hot sterilised jars and seal tightly.

900g/2lb peeled and cored cooking apples, chopped (peeled and cored weight)
225g/8oz onions, peeled and chopped
450g/1lb sultanas
700g/1 $\frac{1}{2}$ lb soft brown sugar
$\frac{1}{4}$ teaspoon salt
900ml/1 $\frac{1}{2}$ pints spiced vinegar (see page 181)

Tropical fruit chutney

Finely dice the pineapple, mango and paw paw (if using) and combine in a small pan with the remaining chutney ingredients. Cook for about 15 minutes over a low heat, stirring regularly, until the mixture thickens to a chutney consistency, without letting it darken too much. Chill. This chutney is designed to be used immediately, however, it will keep in the fridge for a few days.

1 slice of pineapple
$\frac{1}{2}$ mango
$\frac{1}{2}$ paw paw (optional)
5cm/1 inch piece of fresh ginger, grated
1 clove of garlic, peeled and crushed
$\frac{1}{2}$ small red onion, peeled and finely diced
2 tablespoons red wine vinegar
1 tablespoon soft brown sugar
Ground cloves and cumin, to taste

Lemon curd

Put the lemon juice and zest, butter and caster sugar in a large bowl set over a saucepan of simmering water, making sure the water is not touching the base of the bowl. Leave until the butter has melted and the sugar dissolved, stirring occasionally. Lightly whisk the eggs, then pour them on to the mixture through a sieve. Leave for 40 minutes–1 hour, stirring occasionally with a wooden spoon. The curd is ready when it is thick enough to coat the back of the spoon. Remove from the heat, pour into hot sterilised jars and seal tightly.

Juice and grated zest of
  5–6 lemons
225g/8oz unsalted butter,
  diced
275g/10oz caster sugar
10 eggs

'I have a jar of chutney on the table all the time. The chutney varies, but they all seem to go with an enormous variety of foods'

Mustard, mayonnaise and Greek yoghurt dressing

Fast running out of mayo, bank holiday weekend, panic – or rescue as it turned out. So popular was this dressing that customers started to ask for it and we had to quickly remember how we had made it.

Mix all three ingredients.

4 tablespoons mayonnaise

4 tablespoons Greek-style yoghurt

4 tablespoons grainy mustard

French dressing

Everyone has their own French dressing. The proportions vary, as do the ingredients, but this is the combination we find works best for us. Use this as a basis and experiment until you find what works for you.

Place all the ingredients in a bowl and liquidise. This can be stored in a bottle and shaken vigorously before using. It will keep in the fridge for several weeks.

300ml/$\frac{1}{2}$ pint sunflower oil

300ml/$\frac{1}{2}$ pint olive oil

300ml/$\frac{1}{2}$ pint peanut oil

300ml/$\frac{1}{2}$ pint red wine vinegar

Salt and pepper

2 garlic cloves

3 tablespoons grainy mustard

2 dessertspoons honey

Rosemary, garlic and chilli oil

Combine 500ml/15fl oz olive oil, 1 heaped teaspoon dried chilli flakes, 3 sprigs of rosemary and 3 garlic cloves, roughly chopped, in a small saucepan over a low heat. Gently cook for 20 minutes, allow to cool, strain and pour into a bottle. Store in the fridge.

Spiced vinegar

To each 600ml/1 pint of naturally brewed malt vinegar, add 1 level
tablespoon of mixed pickling spice and simmer for 15 minutes.
Strain into hot sterilised bottles and seal tightly.

'A freshly dressed salad is perfect food, light and full of flavour. Ingredients may vary
with the seasons, but it is always the sort of food I want to eat'

SUNDRIES

'Roasting peppers, toasting seeds and nuts, dry-frying spices, these are the kind of culinary lessons that make all the difference'

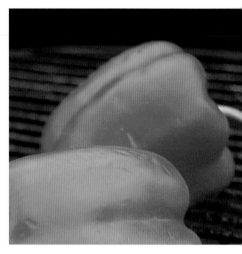

Roasting red peppers, page 185

This is something of a catch-all chapter, home to the bits and pieces that do not belong elsewhere, or belong in more than one place. In many French recipe books this would be the first chapter, where many of the master recipes that go to make up other dishes reside. We have put it at the back on purpose because the kind of food we cook is not really that complicated. We do not build dishes, incorporating other recipes in their construction. Instead we take good ingredients and fashion them with speed and simplicity into something to eat. Our customers are hungry and want nourishing, simple food, not some culinary masterclass.

Our chefs tend to be cooks, not television-starring, multi-restaurant owners in search of another book deal. They cook because they like to, they do it well and enjoy the instant feedback from happy customers. People come to Avoca because they want a bowl of well-made soup, not to work their way through eight courses.

And this is surely the kind of food people generally cook at home. This is the chapter that tells you how to dress a salad, make pastry and fry spices. It is the chapter which will show you how easy it is to cook on a Thursday night; a piece of grilled fish or chicken can be made into a feast with roasted peppers (page 185), a salsa

Shortcrust pastry, page 186

incorporating some dry-fried spices (page 185), or served with a rich tomato sauce, which you happen to have prepared earlier and have in your freezer (page 184). Culinary life does not need to be complicated.

Many large companies look to exercise control, particularly as they grow, but in our case the control is already invested in you, the customer. Tell us you don't like something often enough and it will come off the menu. In truth, most chefs have their own recipe for shortcrust pastry for example, so it will vary depending on whether you are eating in Moll's Gap or Powerscourt. The one given in this chapter is the most widely used but there are variations. That is, we believe, a strength. How dull to eat the same pastry all the time. What is important is that it is good pastry.

This is not a cookery course and some areas have not been covered – roasting meat, for example, or working with eggs. But in an age when cookery books abound, it seemed a tad repetitious to deal with subjects that have been perfectly adequately covered elsewhere. The assumption made is that you want to eat good food and spend a little time preparing it – not hours, but enough time to enjoy a glass of wine and relax.

Tomato sauce

Gently sauté the onions in the olive oil for 10 minutes or until opaque. Add the garlic, cook for 1 minute and then add the chopped tomatoes, wine, sugar and some salt and pepper. Cook over a low heat until reduced in volume by two thirds. Stir in the semi sun-dried tomatoes and basil and check the seasoning.

2 onions, peeled and finely diced
75ml/3fl oz olive oil
6 large garlic cloves, peeled and crushed
2 x 400g/14oz cans of chopped tomatoes
A glass of red wine
A pinch of sugar
50g/2oz semi sun-dried tomatoes
A bunch of basil, chopped

Roux

Melt the butter, add the flour and cook gently for five minutes, taking care that the mixture does not colour. Allow to cool and refrigerate. This will last for a few days if kept covered and can then be added into sauces to thicken them. The roux must be stirred into a hot sauce, otherwise it is likely to form lumps.

50g/2oz butter
50g/2oz plain flour

Variation
White sauce: cook the roux as above and then whisk in 600ml/1pint of full cream milk. Bring to simmering point and cook gently, stirring all the time for 10 minutes. Season with salt, pepper and nutmeg (optional).

Roasting peppers

The object is to char the outside of the peppers really well. Don't be too timid; they should be black. Put the peppers in the top of a hot oven, under the grill or on a barbecue. Turn them only when they have charred. When black all over, transfer to a bowl and cover with clingfilm, or wrap in a damp tea towel. Leave to cool and then remove the skin and seeds. If the peppers are still hot and you are in a hurry, skin them under a cold running tap.

Cooking with spices

As a rule, buy spices whole rather than ground; they keep for much longer and will have a better flavour and aroma. Grind them yourself, using a pestle and mortar or coffee grinder, and then gently warm them in oil so they lose their raw flavour and take on a full, rounded aroma. Alternatively, you can dry-fry whole spices in the same way as seeds (see below) and then grind them. This is particularly useful when using spices uncooked in salads. If you are using your coffee grinder, finish cleaning it with a little bread, it will pick up the last vestiges of coffee or spices.

Toasting nuts and seeds

Nuts, like pine nuts, hazelnuts, almonds, peanuts and cashews, should be spread out on a baking tray and toasted in a moderate oven, 180°C/350°F/gas mark 4. They will take 5–10 minutes, depending on size. They burn very quickly towards the end. Seeds like sesame, poppy, mustard seeds, linseeds, pumpkin and sunflower are best roasted in a dry frying pan to bring out their flavour. Thoroughly heat a frying pan over a moderate heat. Add the seeds and roast for 2–5 minutes, stirring frequently, until lightly browned.

Making croutons and crostini

Slice bread and cut into cubes of the required size, about 1cm/½ inch is usual, but you can make them thicker. Toss in a bowl with oil and fry over a moderate heat until golden brown, tossing frequently. You can add a few crushed cloves of garlic towards the end for flavour if you like. To make crostini, slice a baguette thinly, brush with oil and place under a hot grill. It must be hot – if you grill at too low a temperature your crostini will turn out chewy and rather horrible and your guests will not forgive you!

Pancake batter

Sift the flour into a bowl, then whisk in the eggs, milk, soda water and oil to form a smooth batter. Leave to stand for a few minutes. To make the pancakes, heat a large pancake pan until very hot, lightly smear with oil and then ladle in enough batter to coat the base of the pan thinly, tilting the pan so the mixture spreads evenly. You will probably need a few practice shots before you obtain the correct thickness. Cook over a moderate heat for 1–2 minutes, until golden brown underneath. Then flip the pancake over with a palette knife (or toss it) and cook the second side. Turn out on to greaseproof paper. The pancakes can be made in advance and layered between sheets of greaseproof paper, then wrapped in foil.

275g/10oz plain flour
6 eggs
675ml/23fl oz milk
350ml/12fl oz soda water
1 tablespoon vegetable or
    sunflower oil, plus extra for
    frying

Shortcrust pastry

Everyone swears by their own pastry recipe, so if you have one, stick to it. If, on the other hand, you are a newcomer to pastrymaking or unhappy with your current version, this is the one most widely used throughout the cafés and is passed on with enthusiasm.

Sift the flour into a bowl and rub in the butter until the mixture resembles fine breadcrumbs. Stir in the salt or caster sugar, then mix to a dough with the egg yolks and a little cold water if necessary. Wrap in clingfilm and leave to rest in the fridge for 20–30 minutes. Roll out on a lightly floured work surface and use to line a deep 28cm/11 inch loose-bottomed flan tin.

To bake blind, cover the pastry with greaseproof paper and fill with baking beans (either ceramic ones or any raw dried beans, which you can reuse for baking blind). Bake in an oven preheated to 180°C/350°F/gas mark 4 for 20 minutes. Remove the beans and greaseproof paper and return the pastry case to the oven for 5–10 minutes, until very lightly coloured.

After removing the beans and paper, you could brush the partly cooked pastry with lightly beaten egg white before returning it to the oven. This helps to form a seal and keeps the pastry crisp when you add the filling.

225g/8oz plain flour
150g/5oz butter, diced
$\frac{1}{2}$ teaspoon salt
    (for savoury pastry) or
    25g/1oz caster sugar
    (for sweet pastry)
1–2 egg yolks

'The pastry work at Avoca reminds me so much of my grandmother's – she was the best, no funny stuff, just good honest home baking'

INDEX

My thanks to Simon Pratt, who commissioned the book in the first place and to all at Avoca Handweavers who enthusiastically gave so much of their time and with so much patience as we interrupted, asked questions, rearranged things, took photographs and generally made a nuisance of ourselves. A project like this starts as a gem of an idea and can quickly take over, often to the detriment of normal life. That you all still managed to cook and serve such delicious food to thousands with a smile is no mean feat.

To Leylie Hayes particularly, who with charm, enthusiasm and a wicked sense of humour set out from the beginning to draw all the various strands of the Avoca cafés together. That you managed this mamouth task alongside everything else left me speechless.

The recipes in this book come from all manner or sources, from employees past and present. Where possible we have tried to credit them, if there are errors they were certainly not intentional and I apologise in advance for any made.

My thanks too, go to Vanessa Courtier, who designed the book with such wit and charm, understanding intrinsically from the beginning what we were trying to achieve. Her bold use of white space, her innate understanding of text and sympathetic use of photographs have all combined to bring the book together and make it whole.

The recipe shots, styled by Vanessa and Georgia together, were shot during the summer of 1999 in the grounds of Kilmacanogue, Powerscourt and Avoca. Georgia's innovation and elegance continue to inspire and amaze me.

Hugo Arnold